S0-BJZ-025

Speed and Power

Other Publications:

TIME-LIFE LIBRARY OF CURIOUS AND UNUSUAL FACTS
AMERICAN COUNTRY
VOYAGE THROUGH THE UNIVERSE
THE THIRD REICH
THE TIME-LIFE GARDENER'S GUIDE
MYSTERIES OF THE UNKNOWN
TIME FRAME
FIX IT YOURSELF
FITNESS, HEALTH & NUTRITION
SUCCESSFUL PARENTING
HEALTHY HOME COOKING
LIBRARY OF NATIONS
THE ENCHANTED WORLD
THE KODAK LIBRARY OF CREATIVE PHOTOGRAPHY
GREAT MEALS IN MINUTES
THE CIVIL WAR
PLANET EARTH
COLLECTOR'S LIBRARY OF THE CIVIL WAR
THE EPIC OF FLIGHT
THE GOOD COOK
WORLD WAR II
HOME REPAIR AND IMPROVEMENT
THE OLD WEST

This volume is one of a series that examines
various aspects of computer technology and
the role computers play in modern life.

UNDERSTANDING COMPUTERS

Speed and Power

BY THE EDITORS OF TIME-LIFE BOOKS

TIME-LIFE BOOKS, ALEXANDRIA, VIRGINIA

Contents

7   The Pursuit of Power
     ESSAY   Engine for a Science Revolution   1

31   The Wizard of Chippewa Falls
     ESSAY   Beating Hardware Bottlenecks   2

67   Alternatives to Supercomputers
     ESSAY   Manipulating Massive Models   3

89   The Promise of Parallelism
     ESSAY   Toward Swifter Switching   4

120 Glossary
123 Bibliography
125 Acknowledgments, Picture Credits
126 Index

The Pursuit
of Power

Late in the summer of 1985, in the computer room at Chevron Geosciences Company in Houston, engineers were putting their new Cray X-MP computer system through its paces. At the time, the $10-million machine was one of the fastest computers in the world. To test the reliability of the Cray's circuits, the technicians had given it a problem: Check a series of astronomically large numbers to see if any of them was a prime — a number divisible only by itself and 1. The sleek, cylindrical computer had been working for three hours, quietly performing millions of calculations per second and occasionally printing out its results, when it reported that one of the numbers in the series was indeed a prime. In fact, it was the largest then known — a number whose 65,050 digits, if printed like the type in this book, would cover more than 17 pages.

Discovering primes of this size has little practical utility aside from testing a computer's reliability, but hunting for primes has been a favorite mathematical pastime for millennia. The largest known prime of the precomputer era, with 39 digits, was proved by French mathematician Edouard Lucas in 1876. Much bigger prey came within reach when electronic computers were enlisted in the hunt. In 1952, researchers from the University of California at Los Angeles used a computer to discover a prime with 687 digits. But as the number of digits in a potential prime increases, the computational work required to prove its primeness grows exponentially. The 1.5 trillion calculations needed to prove the Houston prime would have taken more than a year to complete on the swiftest computer available in 1952.

Since the introduction in 1951 of UNIVAC I, the first commercial electronic computer, the speed of the fastest scientific computers has, on the average, doubled every two years. But the goal is not speed for its own sake. A fast computer is a powerful computer: It gives its users a weapon for attacking problems that were once impossibly complex. Chevron's Cray, for example, processes seismic data, manipulating millions of pieces of information with complicated mathematical formulas. The results are used to produce pictures of subterranean formations where oil might be found.

Sorting seismic data is typical of the work performed on the machines known as supercomputers. These systems are seldom given such prosaic jobs as processing payrolls or maintaining mailing lists. Instead, their prodigious calculating abilities are applied to scientific or other problems that can be expressed in mathematical form. Experiments and physical phenomena that are too big, too dangerous, too fast or too slow to study directly can be re-created as masses of numbers and equations for the computer to analyze. Automotive engineers use supercomputers to test new vehicle designs without building expensive prototypes; instead, they crash mathematical cars into mathematical walls. Physicists can study the explosions of nuclear weapons, engineers can probe the safety of nuclear reactors, and aircraft designers can simulate the flow of air over a jet's wings. Chemists can slow the clock, in effect, to watch reactions that take place in tiny fractions of a second, and atmospheric scientists can speed the clock up to study such gradual changes as the build-up of carbon dioxide in the atmosphere.

For computer makers, building a supercomputer is one of the ultimate challenges. In truth, it amounts to multiple challenges. Physicists and engineers develop advanced technology to make the parts of the new machine work faster. Computer architects develop more efficient ways to organize the hundreds or thousands of parts. And software engineers devise lists of instructions, or programs, that will direct the mighty calculating engine in its assigned tasks. The sheer complexity of such a machine guarantees that it will not be cheap. Understandably, many small laboratories and individual scientists cannot afford access to a supercomputer, no matter how much a given problem might demand it. But they may work with computer manufacturers to develop something that is tailored to their situation. The resulting devices include specialized accessories for ordinary computers that produce a big performance boost with only a small cost increase, and inexpensive machines that deliver as much power per dollar as the fastest computers. Such alternatives to supercomputers occupy a growing niche in the market for fast scientific machines.

The first users to seek extraordinary speed from computers — and who were prepared to bear the costs — were agencies of the United States government. The electronic digital computer came into being during World War II, and was used for code breaking and weapons development. In the postwar years, the military found computers indispensable. The design and testing of nuclear weapons, for example, required enormous computing power. In 1954, the fastest computer available spent a hundred hours running through the computations needed to simulate a single nuclear explosion.

This performance did not satisfy scientists at the nation's major nuclear research facilities, the Los Alamos Scientific Laboratory in New Mexico and the University of California Radiation Laboratory at Livermore (renamed Lawrence Radiation Laboratory in 1958, Lawrence Livermore Laboratory in 1971 and Lawrence Livermore National Laboratory in 1981). In 1955, the U. C. Radiation Lab requested proposals for a machine a hundred times faster than any existing computer. IBM and Sperry Rand's Univac Division — the leading computer makers of the day — both submitted bids. Univac got the nod (in part because the firm promised quicker delivery) and immediately began designing a computer that took its name from the customer's location; it was called LARC, for Livermore Advanced Research Computer. Design specifications for LARC were finished in March 1956. They called for less than the hundredfold speed improvement originally envisioned, but with a stringent reliability requirement: The new machine would have to be up and running at least 90 percent of the time.

The LARC designers relied on proven technology for many components of the machine, such as the memory (where information is stored during processing). There were, however, a few important exceptions. Most previous computers had used vacuum tubes as the electronic switches at the heart of their logic circuits, where the actual computing is done. But vacuum tubes were bulky and hot, and they eventually burned out like light bulbs, corrupting results or halting the machine. The alternative was transistors, just then becoming available. Faster at switching than tubes, the smaller, cooler transistors also promised greater reliability. Univac had been looking for a chance to explore this area of electronics

An early step in the quest for greater computing speeds, this motor-driven number sieve built in 1932 tested 300,000 numbers per minute in an effort to sift out a prime — a number divisible only by 1 and itself. A number sieve built of modern electronic components can perform identical mathematical searches at the rate of 100 million tests per second.

and saw the LARC project as a perfect opportunity. With 60,000 transistors, LARC was one of the first computers of any size to incorporate the new technology.

Another important innovation appearing in LARC would soon find wider application. LARC actually consisted of two separate computers: While one performed the numerical computations of a problem, the other handled the processing involved in receiving information from the external world and sending back computed results. Called an input/output controller, this second unit greatly reduced computing time by relieving the main processor of the trafficking work.

Production of LARC fell behind schedule and costs mounted as engineers struggled with such problems as the complex wiring needed to connect the machine's host of transistors. Computer programs were developed to help the designers by determining the most efficient juxtaposition of components and by describing wiring interconnections. The dependability of this untried electronic assistance was a matter of debate; some engineers even resigned from the project to avoid being associated with what they saw as a certain failure. Special techniques and tools were devised for working with the wiring, which in some parts of the machine formed a tangle up to two inches thick. The chief engineer for LARC, Herman Lukoff, wrote later that the workroom looked less like an electronics laboratory than like a hospital operating room, complete with surgical instruments. Fortunately, Lukoff recalled, "the wire men weren't aware of the fact that it couldn't be done, so they went right ahead and completed the work."

LARC was more than four years in the making, almost twice the time specified in the original contract. But late delivery was just about the only deviation from the specifications; when the computer was put to work on nuclear weapons problems in 1960, Livermore scientists pronounced it a technical triumph.

The success was not without its price, however. Few customers for the machine existed — only one additional LARC was built, ordered by the U.S. Navy in 1961 — and Univac had strained its engineering staff to the limit. For its trouble, the company lost an estimated $17 million in unreimbursed development costs. Despite LARC's technological legacy for future Univac computers, the company backed out of the high-stakes race to build the most powerful machines. Chief engineer Lukoff, who stayed with Univac to direct advanced research, later cited LARC's cautionary lesson: "Don't push the state of the art before it is ready to be pushed or else be prepared to pay a price you don't expect."

A STRETCH FOR BIG BLUE
IBM, undeterred by the loss of the Livermore contract in 1955, won a similar contract in 1956 with the Los Alamos Scientific Laboratory. The agreement called for IBM, collaborating with Los Alamos scientists, to build a state-of-the-art computer a hundred times faster than the most powerful machine then available, IBM's own 704. From their research, IBM engineers knew that they could increase performance by a factor of 10 using mostly off-the-shelf components; increasing by a factor of 100 would require new components, improved manufacturing techniques and different design approaches. Everyone involved knew the project would severely tax IBM's engineering resources: Although the proposed machine was officially named the 7030, it was known to its makers — and later, to the world — as Stretch.

Like LARC, Stretch was intended to operate with transistors. But to meet the contract specifications, Stretch engineers would have to create new transistors that were faster than any then available. IBM decided to make the transistors itself, but it took so long in developing the manufacturing capacity that the first lot of the devices had to be supplied by a subcontractor. The next step, building circuits with the transistors, was complicated by a staff of engineers who had cut their teeth on vacuum tubes; to wean them of old habits, a rule was established forbidding anyone to have a vacuum-tube device visible in a work area.

TRICKS OF MEMORY

Improvements in the computer's memory also helped make Stretch faster. The latest high-speed memory cores, tiny metal donuts that held instructions and data in the form of magnetic fields, could feed information to the processing unit within two microseconds—six times as fast as the memory of the 704. (A microsecond is a millionth of a second.) But even this was deemed not fast enough. So the designers borrowed a time-saving technique Univac had incorporated in the LARC. They arranged memory in multiple banks: Information called from successive banks could be overlapped in transit, cutting the average wait for new instructions or data to just half a microsecond.

The electronic complexity required to perform this feat and many others posed huge problems. Because the components were interdependent, any design change might require compensating changes in untold numbers of other parts. Traditionally, IBM's computer designs were recorded on paper by hand, but chief engineer Stephen Dunwell realized that Stretch held far too much wiring to continue this process: The enormous volume of drawings would need so many corrections that it would be almost impossible to get all of them right. As the LARC designers did to untangle their jumble of circuits, the Stretch team turned to a computer, devising a design process that ran on an IBM 704. To simplify the manufacture of circuits for Stretch's 169,100 transistors, IBM had a subcontractor make a machine that could automatically connect some of the wiring in Stretch subassemblies. As Dunwell later said, "We knew we would never get it together if we didn't automate the design and the manufacture."

In many instances, the new technology had wrinkles that needed ironing out, and all of this took time. Stretch was delivered to Los Alamos in April 1961, almost a year late, and nearly five years after the contract signing. And although users at Los Alamos thought highly of the machine and would use it for a decade, Stretch did not measure up to the speed goals of the contract. It was unquestionably the world's fastest computer, with the most complex circuitry yet attempted, but some of the hardware never quite worked the way it was intended. Accounts of the speed discrepancy varied, but one member of the design team estimated that Stretch was only 25 times faster than the 704.

The new technology also cost a bundle. About the time that Stretch was delivered to Los Alamos, IBM's chairman, Thomas J. Watson Jr., announced that the company had drastically underestimated what it would have to spend on building the computer. The government contract covered only a fraction of IBM's total investment in the project, Watson said. The price quoted to other customers for Stretch was reduced from $13.5 million to $8 million, reflecting the performance shortfall. But because the company would lose money on every machine it sold at this price, orders would be taken only through May 15, 1961. "We will make delivery of the machines because we do not want to break our promise to our customers," Watson told the press. "We are going to take a good, fat loss on Stretch." The loss was reported to be $20 million, with a total of eight machines sold, mostly for military-related applications in Europe and the United States. Within IBM, the project was considered a disaster; its principal managers — and indeed the very idea of building supercomputers — fell into temporary disfavor.

Thus the early 1960s saw the top management of the two leading computer manufacturers backing warily away from a market that looked more and more like a morass. Both concentrated instead on building and selling business-oriented computers; demand for these machines had grown steadily through the 1950s, with little sign of falling off in the future.

The absence of IBM and Univac left the door open for an upstart company from Minneapolis. From its inception, Control Data Corporation (CDC) focused on big scientific machines. Founded in 1957, CDC hit the ground running: Its first computer, the transistorized 1604, was unveiled in October 1959 and was faster than the IBM 704. Although the 1604 was soon eclipsed by LARC and Stretch, CDC did not slacken its pace. For most of the next two decades, its computers were to be the standard by which fast machines were judged.

If the company was a brand new player in the computer industry, its managers and engineers were not. Many had gotten their start with a little-known company called Engineering Research Associates (ERA), founded at the dawn of the com-

A trio of IBM executives — among them chief engineer Stephen Dunwell *(center)* — examines a scale model of the company's Stretch 7030 super-computer on the eve of its unveil-ing at the IBM plant in Poughkeepsie, New York, in 1960. Behind them stands the machine itself, its con-sole visible at right.

puter age. ERA was the brainchild of a group of U.S. Navy reserve officers who had served together in a top-secret code-breaking unit during World War II. Two members of this group were William Norris and Howard Engstrom. At war's end, they voiced the idea of forming a company to build cryptographic equipment. They did not really expect to be taken seriously, but their colleagues were receptive, and the navy — eager to retain the services of these technical experts — promised to support their work with contracts if they could find private financing.

The backing came from John E. Parker, a successful investment banker who was a graduate of the Naval Academy and well known to many navy officers. During the war, Parker had established a large factory in St. Paul, Minnesota, to build wooden gliders used in airborne assaults. The demand for gliders ended with the war, and Parker was seeking a new use for the facility. In January 1946, Engineering Research Associates was incorporated in St. Paul. The technical group, led by Norris and Engstrom, owned one half; investors led by Parker, who was named president of the new company, owned the other half.

ERA began making computers and other electronic devices under contract to the navy and the air force. Its first general-purpose machine, Task 13 in its series of navy contracts, was code-named Atlas, for a comic-strip mental giant. Atlas was delivered to the navy in 1950, after three years of development, and was so successful that the company requested permission to market it commercially. The navy agreed to the release of a modified version.

The commercial model was designated the ERA 1101, a name derived from the navy task number — 1101 being the binary representation of the number 13. Among its innovations were an advanced form of memory, built-in air conditioning to cool its vacuum tubes, and a maintenance panel that identified areas of malfunction. But ERA's background as a hardware supplier to the mili-

Control Data president William Norris shows off the company's model 3600 computer in 1964. Until it was surpassed by its speedier cousin, the 6600, the 3600 was the fastest computer in the world.

tary was obvious: When the 1101 was announced in late 1951, the company could offer potential buyers no software and only minimal facilities for getting information in and out of the computer. Putting the computer to work would be the user's problem.

AN UNDERCAPITALIZED SUCCESS

Despite its technical successes and strong sales to the military—by 1952 ERA machines made up an estimated 80 percent of the market value of all U.S. computers—ERA was not home free. The company had little capital to develop new equipment or to provide the services that commercial customers required. Rather than borrow money or issue stock, John Parker began looking for a prospective buyer. He was approached by Remington Rand, a company best known as a manufacturer of typewriters and electric shavers. In 1950, Remington Rand had entered the computer industry by buying the company that built Univac; now it hoped to solidify its leadership position with a new purchase.

Discussions between the two companies were complicated by the fact that Remington Rand's top executives lacked military security clearances. They could be told about the ERA 1101 computer, but because most of ERA's projects were secret, other information about the company could not be disclosed. In these unusual circumstances, the sale price of $1.7 million was finally arrived at by putting a price of $5,000 on the head of each of ERA's 340 engineers. The sale gave Norris and the other original ERA shareholders a profit amounting to 85 times their initial investment. But Norris and his colleagues had decidedly mixed feelings about the takeover. At a Christmas meeting after the consummation of the sale in 1952, Norris handed out electric shavers to his management personnel in place of the usual Christmas turkey.

Bill Norris had a hard time adjusting to Remington Rand. He was made a vice president of the parent company and general manager of ERA operations in St. Paul, but he chafed under the weight of the bureaucracy. His brusque manner and blunt approach to problems irritated James Rand, who was himself something of an autocrat. Norris, for his part, could scarcely disguise his contempt for what he considered incompetent management by executives who knew nothing about computers. There was some justification for his feelings; Remington Rand's financial and management resources were not up to the challenge of maintaining leadership in an industry that changed as fast as it grew. The edge provided by the technical superiority of Univac and ERA was squandered.

In 1955, Remington Rand merged with the larger Sperry Gyroscope Company, and Norris was given charge of the new Sperry Rand Univac Division, which combined all computer operations—and which soon began work on the LARC project. Still subject to the whims and budget decisions of top management in New York, Norris found his frustration mounting. Years later, he still railed at the "confusion, indecision, conflicting orders, organization line breaches, constant organizational change, fighting and unbridled competition between divisions." To Norris, the lesson was clear. "To run a computer company," he said later, "it's necessary to have top executives who understand computers. People are afraid of what they don't understand, and losing money makes a man doubly afraid. Top management in the conglomerates doesn't understand computers, and when the division is losing money, they won't take risks."

In mid-1957, Norris decided to strike out on his own. With a handful of engineers from the old ERA days, he quit Sperry Rand and established the Control Data Corporation in the second-floor offices of an old newspaper warehouse in Minneapolis. The group had experience and expertise — but little else. CDC's cash shortage was remedied somewhat by a public stock offering of $600,000, which sold out almost instantly. Among the 300 or so investors were several former ERA colleagues, left behind at Sperry Rand in St. Paul.

Under Norris, the new company had a simple mandate: "to build large, scientific computers with a lot more bang for the buck." CDC would sell to nonbusiness customers such as the military and other government agencies, private research centers and universities. In particular, Norris courted government research and development funds: During its first five years, CDC sold 70 percent of its computers to the U.S. government. By specializing in fast scientific machines and bypassing business for the time being, Norris hoped to avoid a head-on confrontation with IBM and Sperry Rand. This niche also offered other advantages. Control Data would not require a large sales force: Norris and his colleagues already had many valuable contacts in the military and government, and they could deal with them on a scientist-to-scientist basis. Such customers, moreover, seldom demanded the kind of technical support that was IBM's strongest suit. Many actually preferred the challenge of writing their own programs, obviating the need for CDC to supply software.

The navy helped the company stay afloat by placing an order for a planned machine designated the 1604. Even with that contract in hand, it was a close call. Before the computer was completed, finances got so tight that Norris cut everyone's salary in half to make certain the cash would last to finish the project. The new machine was delivered in 1960, and it proved fast and reliable. One of the first fully transistorized computers available on the commercial market, it sold for slightly less than one million dollars, a low price for a machine that could be used for large, complex problems in fields such as nuclear physics. Even the computer's name, 1604, reflected its ERA heritage: It was said to have been arrived at by adding 1103 — the name of the last computer ERA produced for Sperry Rand — to the numerals in Control Data's Minneapolis address, 501 Park Avenue.

A SINGLE-MINDED GENIUS

The designer of the 1604 was the company's young vice president of engineering, Seymour R. Cray, who had been with Norris since ERA days. Cray was a creative genius, and he knew exactly what he wanted to do with his life — build the world's most powerful computers. But he hated his administrative responsibilities and the distractions of the office. He owned land near his hometown of Chippewa Falls, Wisconsin, and yearned to work there, nearly a hundred miles from Minneapolis. The flinty Norris might have shown a lesser employee the door, but Cray was one of his company's greatest assets. Avoiding a potential crisis, Norris agreed to build a one-story lab near Cray's home, on a wooded bluff overlooking the Chippewa River.

Early in 1962, Cray moved into this sylvan setting and began work on the fast computer of his dreams, which would be called the 6600. This was a major undertaking, financed in part by a multimillion-dollar deal with the Atomic Energy Commission's Lawrence Radiation Laboratory, which still had its LARC

Color-coded skeins of wire spill from two of the four cabinets that made up Control Data's 6600 supercomputer. The wires varied in length so as to synchronize the arrival of electrical impulses traveling along them. The copper tubes at lower right carried a refrigerant to cool the machine.

(and a Stretch as well) but was looking for something even more powerful. Cray's working methods were totally unlike the approach used by IBM and Univac. His staff numbered only 34, including the night janitor. Cray did much of the wire soldering himself, often working through the lunch hour — he carried his lunch in a metal pail like a construction worker — and sometimes far into the night. No one visited the lab without an appointment, including the boss himself. Norris came twice a year, and Cray made the trip to Minneapolis every six weeks or so.

Development of the 6600 was far enough along by August 1963 — some 18 months after Cray's move to the woods — to invite the press to view it. Outside the Chippewa Falls lab, reporters saw a salt lick for deer; inside was an electronic marvel. It was almost 14 feet long and more than six feet high, with 80 miles of circuitry. The computer's 350,000 transistors — so densely packed that air could not circulate — were cooled by a special refrigerant flowing through

copper tubes *(page 35)*. The machine had 10 peripheral processors, small computers that fed instructions and data to the extremely fast central processor, which could execute three million instructions per second. The 6600 was 20 times faster than the CDC 1604 and three times faster than IBM's Stretch, which was no longer in production. So great was the computer's power that some of Cray's engineers confessed they could scarcely conceive of problems complex enough to challenge it.

Publicity for the 6600 sent Control Data's stock soaring. CDC was the newest sensation in the electronics industry and a darling of Wall Street. One place where the announcement was not well received, however, was at IBM, by now the undisputed leader of the computer industry. Chief executive Watson was outraged at being shown up by this Minnesota midget. In a scathing memo to his top seven executives in August 1963, Watson referred to press accounts of Cray's minimal staff: "Contrasting this modest effort with our own vast development activities, I fail to understand why we have lost our industry leadership position by letting someone else offer the world's most powerful computer."

ORDERS FROM THE TOP

The following month, Watson convened his annual meeting of senior management. One participant recalled the meeting's explosive atmosphere: "The salespeople were saying they couldn't hold the line against CDC. The engineers were bitching about our lack of advanced technology, and the research people wanted more money. Tom just said, 'I want a machine. I refuse to be second best.' " The participant added, "When we killed Stretch, we sank our flagship, but nobody liked to remind Tom of that." Watson created a task force to build a machine that could outpace Control Data's 6600. The starting point was Project X, a previously low-priority research program aiming at a computer 10 times more powerful than Stretch. After Stretch's demise, the project had been kept alive by a core group of engineers who preferred the challenge of building supercomputers to the task of designing IBM's bread-and-butter payroll processors.

In its eagerness to show up Control Data, IBM announced the "ultra-high performance" Model 90 in August 1964, before engineers had even produced a prototype. Intended to be the top of the line in IBM's new System/360 computer series, the Model 90 was touted as faster than the 6600. The mere announcement that IBM was back in the supercomputer field caused several customers to abandon plans to order the 6600. And IBM's sales staff created uncertainty among other potential Control Data customers by privately talking up the superiority of a Model 90 supercomputer that did not yet exist.

Control Data's prospects were further darkened by delays in getting the 6600 into service: Eliminating the last bugs proved to be more difficult than Cray had anticipated. The first machine, scheduled for delivery to the Lawrence Radiation Laboratory in February 1964, was not installed until August. Then troubles with transistors cropped up in 1965, when 6600s were delivered to a half dozen other big customers, including the U.S. Air Force and the Weather Bureau. The same year, difficulties in manufacturing the machine in quantity developed when Norris transferred production from Chippewa Falls to a plant in St. Paul.

Although problems with the 6600 were the most worrisome — Norris later admitted that he was "betting the future of the company" on it — CDC had other woes, most of them related to the firm's rapid growth. By 1964, the company was producing a variety of computers for business in addition to its scientific machines. But Control Data got caught in a price war in the market for smaller computers, and Norris—in a move he later ascribed to panic—extended his price cuts by lopping two million dollars off the average six-million-dollar price tag on the 6600. Meanwhile, Norris had acquired several companies that manufactured peripheral equipment·needed to support computers, and many of these firms were losing money. Further financial pressure came from the increasing tendency of Control Data's customers to lease rather than buy computers. Customers facing rapidly changing technology were thus spared being stuck with out-of-date machines, but because it no longer got full payment for its computers on delivery, Control Data had to wait longer to recoup its costs.

Things looked so bad by early 1966 that when the company borrowed $120 million, rumors of impending bankruptcy raced through Wall Street. But Bill Norris persevered. Born and raised on a Nebraska farm, he liked to tell doubters a story about returning to run the farm after he had graduated from college and failed to find a job. Drought was burning all the crops in the summer of 1934 and many farmers, convinced that the dwindling supplies of grain and hay would not be enough to get their cattle through the winter, were selling the animals. Norris decided he could get his own livestock through by feeding them the only green thing in sight, Russian thistles, mixed with cottonseed cake. And gambling that the spring would bring nourishing rain, he even bought other farmers' cattle. "We moved and stacked more than a hundred acres of green Russian thistles," Norris remembered. "I had difficulty finding people to help because no one wanted the onus of being involved in such a foolhardy enterprise."

In the parable, of course, Norris's faith was vindicated. The·cattle survived the winter on thistles and cottonseed cake, and the spring rains came. Now, more than three decades later, his risk-taking paid off again. The companies he had acquired began making money, and the 6600 shook off its bugs and lived up to expectations. Before the decade was out, orders for the machine would pass the hundred mark. With confidence restored on Wall Street, Control Data's roller-coaster common stock shot skyward again; by 1967, Norris' own $75,000 investment in 1957 had a paper worth of some $55.5 million. And in 1968 Norris solved Control Data's continuing cash-flow problem by purchasing a large finance company, Commercial Credit, whose $3.4 billion in working assets could provide ample capital for building and leasing computers.

The success of the 6600 contrasted sharply with the fate of the Model 90 supercomputer IBM had announced back in 1964. Plagued by technical dif-

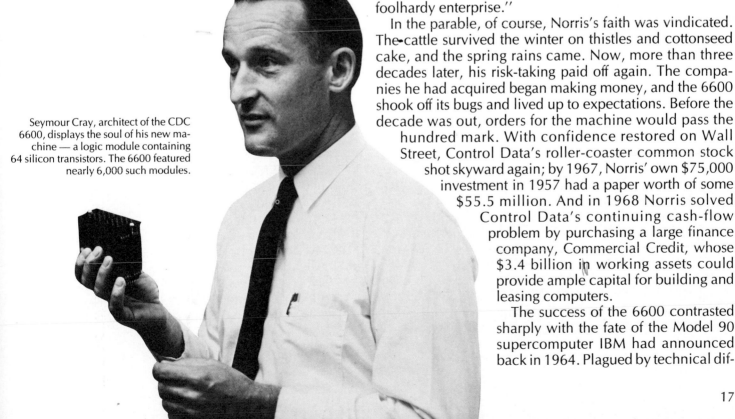

Seymour Cray, architect of the CDC 6600, displays the soul of his new machine — a logic module containing 64 silicon transistors. The 6600 featured nearly 6,000 such modules.

ficulties, IBM kept changing the specifications, the design and even the numerical designation of the original Model 90, announcing four different versions. The first machine was not delivered until 1967. In the same year, IBM announced that it had always considered the computer a "limited project" and would accept no more orders. Only a dozen more were sold. This venture into supercomputing was even more costly than its forerunner, Stretch; although the Model 90, like Stretch, provided technological benefits for later IBM machines, the company lost an estimated $126 million on the project.

Norris was infuriated by the whole Model 90 episode. Convinced that IBM's premature announcement of its machine was unethical if not illegal, he pressed his board of directors to bring a lawsuit against the computer giant. Filed in December 1968, the suit charged IBM with 37 instances of attempting to monopolize the computer industry. Central to these charges was the supercomputer episode. To deter customers from ordering the 6600, the suit alleged, IBM had marketed "paper machines and phantom computers," machines "not yet in production, and as to which it had no reasonable basis for believing that production or delivery could be accomplished within the time periods specified."

A LUCRATIVE OUTCOME

It was a real David and Goliath confrontation; in 1968, IBM was worth nearly $7 billion to Control Data's $438 million. Norris later recalled that some of his board members opposed the suit out of fear that "IBM would just turn around and kick the hell out of Control Data." But that scenario never came to pass. After five years of litigation, the suit was settled out of court. IBM agreed to pay Control Data a package of cash and other subsidies worth $101 million. In addition, IBM agreed to sell CDC its subsidiary, Service Bureau Corporation, thus enabling Control Data to become a leading vendor of data-processing services. The subsidiary was sold at book value, considered a bargain price. It was estimated that, after paying legal and other expenses, Control Data came out of the litigation nearly $100 million ahead. Norris, once again vindicated as well as victorious, called the suit "one of the best management decisions in our history."

For supercomputer users, however, Control Data's victory over IBM was sealed not in court, but in Seymour Cray's lab overlooking the Chippewa River. Even as the legal battle was being joined in December 1968, reporters trekked through the snow to "Seymour's Place" for a first viewing of a handsome new machine. Shaped like a hollow square of cabinets paneled in walnut and blue glass, it was the CDC 7600, a successor to the 6600 that offered five times the speed at only twice the price. Cray and his organization had learned the lessons of the 6600 well; the 7600 suffered few of the problems that had tormented the earlier machine. Vastly more powerful than the top products of other companies, the 7600 quickly attracted a queue of interested customers, led by that perennial consumer of computing power, the Lawrence Radiation Laboratory. For the next decade, no serious challenger would threaten Control Data's position as the preeminent builder of the very fastest scientific computers. And when a contender for the crown finally appeared, it came not from IBM or Univac in New York, but from a brand-new company in, of all places, Chippewa Falls.

Engine for a Science Revolution

Scientists and engineers have always relied on the language of mathematics to explain physical phenomena and make predictions from theory, whether forecasting the path of a planet or estimating the strength of a trusswork bridge. Often, however, they have been in the frustrating position of possessing all the mathematical tools needed to solve a problem without being able to exploit them — simply because of the amount of computational work involved. For example, the equations that describe fluid dynamics — the flow of water around a ship's hull or of air over a plane's wing — have been known since the 1820s. But until recently, using the equations to evaluate a hull or wing design would have been so time-consuming that engineers instead could only try out their ideas empirically, building models and running them through test-tank or wind-tunnel trials. Supercomputers have changed that.

Anything that can be described numerically is grist for a computer, and today's fastest machines can manipulate numbers at a rate that compresses a lifetime's worth of pencil-and-paper calculations into perhaps a second. Such number-crunching prowess is now being put to work on all sorts of scientific and engineering frontiers. Geophysicists use supercomputers to figure out the patterns of circulation in the world's oceans or the buildup of carbon dioxide in the atmosphere. Astronomers trace the ways the universe cooled after its genesis in a stupendous explosion about 15 billion years ago. Automobile designers mathematically explore the combustion of various fuel mixtures in an engine or the buckling of sheet metal in a collision.

Such computerized problem solving poses some formidable challenges, however. It generally depends on constructing a very elaborate mathematical model — a set of equations that accounts for whatever is under investigation. Success also depends on writing a program that will run this model efficiently. And a sophisticated graphics program is then needed to express the numerical results in a visual form that the human mind can comprehend. All of the preparatory intellectual labor can take months or even years. But the resulting insights are often so useful that supercomputers are said to have wrought a second scientific revolution.

Probing the Microworld

No eye is keen enough, no microscope powerful enough, to see into the heart of an atom. But by harnessing the speed of a supercomputer, scientists can simulate the behavior of molecules, atoms, even subatomic particles. This computational process, a marriage of chemistry and physics, starts with a mathematical description of the matter under scrutiny. The equations of quantum mechanics are used if chemical reactions or the structure of molecules are being studied; other approaches serve for such purposes as determining the mo-

The computational chemist starts with an image of the substances to be mathematically simulated. At left is an artist's rendition of a small part of the protein molecule myoglobin, including an atom of iron and a water molecule (purple spheres). The structure was determined by X-ray diffraction analysis, a technique that involves bombarding a substance with X-rays and studying the scatter pattern. The data gained from such an analysis serves as the basis for a mathematical model.

tions of atoms at a given temperature. By solving groups of such equations, researchers can gain new insights into molecular architecture, follow the course of lightning-quick interactions, and even predict the properties of compounds that have yet to be created.

The difficulty lies in the complexity of the equations involved. Even relatively simple chemicals may have many electrons per molecule (water, for example, has 10), and each of those electrons will be affected from moment to moment by the others and also by the atomic nuclei. To simulate each moment of a chemical process therefore requires the solution of a so-called many-body problem for many different arrangements of the atoms. For reactions that take place in no more than 10^{-12} second, this complicated effort must be repeated 500 or even 1,000 times. But the payoff is potentially enormous. Computational chemistry seems certain to lead to new drugs, lubricants, plastics and other materials for tomorrow's world.

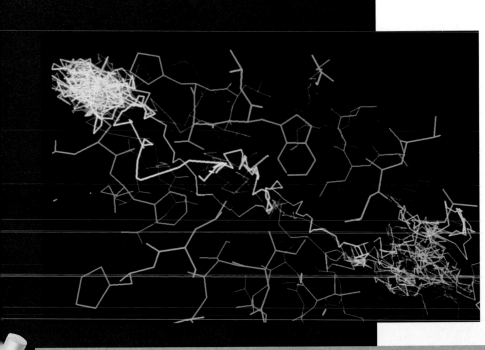

This computer-generated picture shows four of the one million paths that might be followed by electrons streaming through myoglobin. Once scientists refined the algorithm to produce the simulation, performing the calculations took a University of Illinois supercomputer about three hours. A full-scale analysis of electron movement in myoglobin would require an algorithm capable of dealing with the molecule's 2,500 atoms and thousands of electrons.

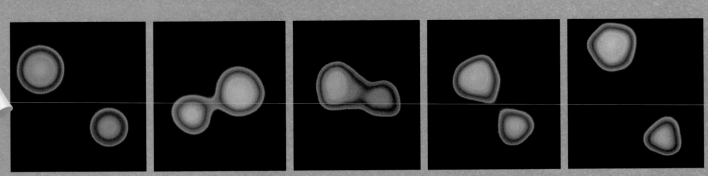

The Course of a Nuclear Collision

A krypton nucleus collides with a lanthanum nucleus in these images from the graphic output of a supercomputer simulation. The sequence is what physicists call a deep inelastic event. The nuclei do not shatter into subatomic smithereens as they would in a head-on central collision, nor do they glance lightly off each other as in a peripheral collision. Instead, they meet with enough force to briefly squeeze themselves together into a super-heavy nucleus, which then splits in two, yielding fragments that differ only by a few neutrons and protons from the original pair. The mathematics is so complex that researchers spent a year figuring out the best way to do the computations. A Cray-1 did them in 90 minutes. In the real world, this sequence would take place in 10^{-21} second.

Computerized Flight Testing

Supercomputers have become indispensable in the design of aircraft, mathematically simulating airflow patterns that determine such critical performance factors as lift, drag and stability. Previously, the only way aeronautical engineers could see how their creations would perform was to build models of portions of the craft, typically at a cost of about $100,000 apiece, and test them in a wind tunnel. As much as $50 million could be spent on wind-tunnel testing of a single new design. Expense was only one drawback of this proce-

The first step in modeling aircraft for computerized test flight is to lay a mesh or grid over an image of the craft and its surrounding space. The idealized representation at right is, in practice, refined to conform to the shape of the craft — in this case, the space shuttle shown below. A set of fluid-dynamics equations is then used to calculate the behavior of air particles streaming past each of the intersection points at each instant of time.

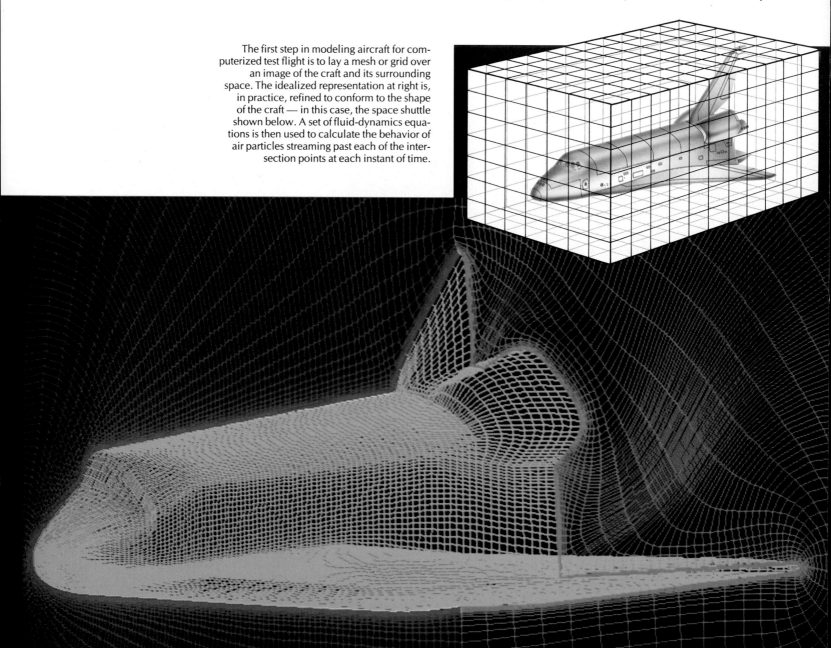

dure: No wind-tunnel test could perfectly match flight reality, since the walls of the tunnel and the supports for the model would inevitably cause distortions in the airflow.

A supercomputer can evaluate designs much more quickly and cheaply — and also without distortions. But its mathematical mimicry is far from simple. One program used by engineers works out the pressure, density and velocity of flowing air at 100,000 separate points on or near the aircraft. To solve fluid-dynamics equations for these values at a single instant of time requires about 50 billion operations.

Aircraft designers still consider wind-tunnel testing essential to verify their conclusions. But by flying mathematical models in a computer, they can try out many more design possibilities. The computer can also simulate conditions that no wind tunnel can match, such as flying an aircraft at many times the speed of sound or in the rarified upper reaches of the atmosphere—both expected to be routine feats for the airliners of the twenty-first century.

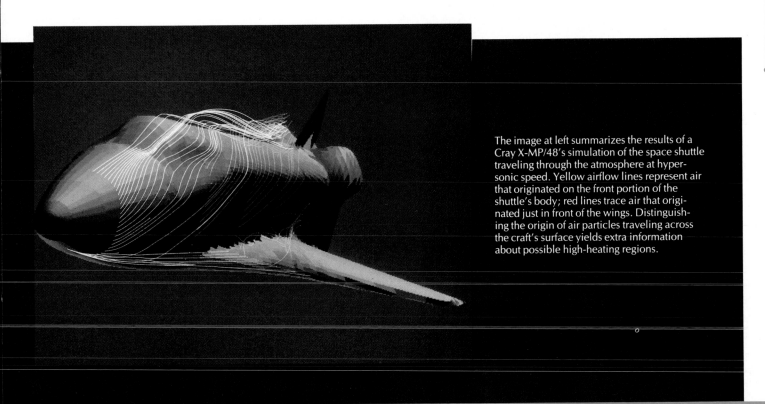

The image at left summarizes the results of a Cray X-MP/48's simulation of the space shuttle traveling through the atmosphere at hypersonic speed. Yellow airflow lines represent air that originated on the front portion of the shuttle's body; red lines trace air that originated just in front of the wings. Distinguishing the origin of air particles traveling across the craft's surface yields extra information about possible high-heating regions.

Trying Out a Wing Design

A simulated business jet soars in a supercomputer test flight, its color-coded surface representing differences in the pressure and velocity of air particles passing across every part of the plane's exterior. The purpose of the simulation — based on a mathematical model for 5,400 discrete points on the plane's surface — was to analyze the airflow around the combined mass of each wing and engine housing. A Cray X-MP/24 supercomputer took about 23 minutes to carry out the calculations needed to produce this image. If the results had been unsatisfactory, the aircraft would have been mathematically redesigned and retested in the computer.

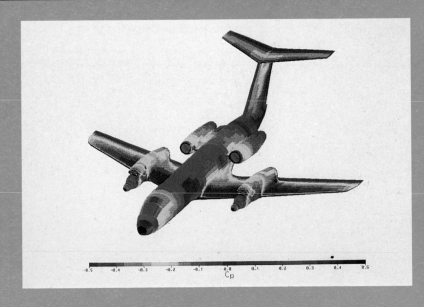

23

A Computer-Guided Restoration

When engineers set about restoring the Statue of Liberty for her 100th birthday in 1986, they plotted their labors with a computerized technique called finite-element analysis, which was used for tasks as diverse as designing a bridge or predicting the handling abilities of a new automobile. In finite-element analysis, a structure is broken down into many small shapes — triangles, rectangles, cylinders, blocks or any other geometric form. Points where the elements meet are called nodes, and the structure's mass is treated as though

The computer-generated color image at left uncovers the skeleton of the Statue of Liberty — iron columns, struts and brackets normally hidden beneath 32 tons of copper skin. At right is a so-called dynamic model of the statue, consisting of a multitude of finite-element shapes that are analyzed to replicate the structure's response to forces and loads. The dots, known as lumped mass points, are a mathematical simplification of the statue's distribution of mass.

it were concentrated at a few discrete positions. The role of the computer is to calculate how the forces affect each element and how each element affects its neighbors — a job that typically requires solving tens of thousands of simultaneous equations. By manipulating the model, engineers can move sections of a structure, add or subtract supporting members, identify weight-bearing elements and test the results of hypothetical adjustments. The engineers can also subject the structure to endurance tests by entering equations into the computer that simulate wind pressure or sudden impact.

Among other revelations, the finite-element analysis of the Statue of Liberty showed exactly why she sometimes waved her torch so much in the wind that one of the spikes on her crown pierced her arm. Owing to a deviation from the statue's original design by French engineer Gustave Eiffel, structural members in the shoulder were subjected to bending stresses that they were not intended to carry. A supercomputer guided the repair.

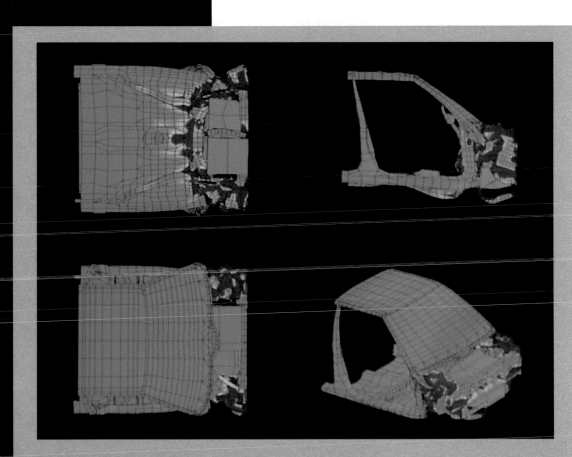

An Exercise in Metal-Bending

Automobile makers in earlier years used to crash-test their new car designs by building prototypes and driving them into walls. Today, a supercomputer can perform a finite-element analysis in order to predict how each part of a vehicle would fare in the event of a head-on collision. The four images above,

for example, depict a 35-mile-per-hour crash simulation that was run on a Cray X-MP. The mathematical model had nearly 8,000 elements connected at almost 7,000 nodes. Dark red areas highlight those portions of the automobile that suffered the most stress during the simulated accident.

Sounding the Depths for Oil

Supercomputers are hard at work in the energy business, helping out with jobs that range from designing nuclear power plants to hunting for oil beneath the sea. As an oil-seeking tool, both on land and at sea, the computer's role is to make sense of the mountains of data generated by a technique called seismic imaging — the use of sound waves to create a picture of rock formations and sedimentary layers where hydrocarbons may hide.

air gun

hydrophones

A ship conducting a seismic study of the seabed travels a planned route back and forth across the survey area, firing periodic blasts of sound energy downward from towed air guns. The answering echoes are picked by a towed string of hydrophones, each one recording the reflections for later analysis by computer. The blasts of low-frequency sound are so powerful that echoes can be detected from a depth of 15 kilometers within the earth's crust.

To gather the raw data for a marine seismic image, geologists fire carefully timed bursts of low-frequency sound from air guns towed behind a ship proceeding back and forth over a survey area. The sound waves travel down through the water to the seabed, which reflects most of the sound back toward the surface. Some of the sonic energy, however, passes through the ocean floor and into the rock layers below. Each successive layer reflects a portion of the remaining sound, sending up a series of progressively fainter and more garbled echoes. All of the echoes are picked up by a string of hydrophones towed aft of the air guns. The timing and strength of the reflected sounds hold clues to the thickness and composition of the layers — but hours of supercomputer number-crunching are needed to sift out distortions and noise and transform the cacophony into a comprehensible geological portrait.

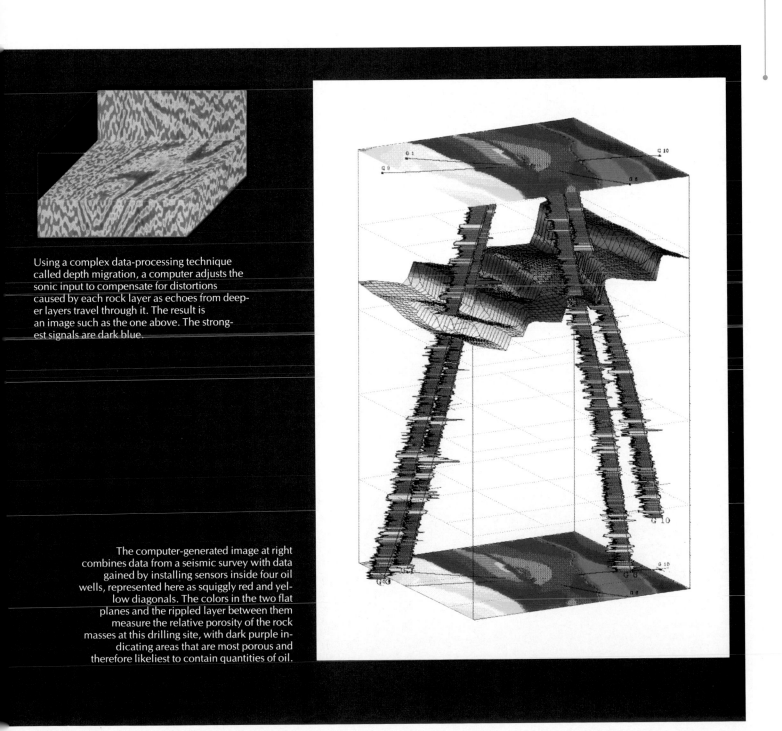

Using a complex data-processing technique called depth migration, a computer adjusts the sonic input to compensate for distortions caused by each rock layer as echoes from deeper layers travel through it. The result is an image such as the one above. The strongest signals are dark blue.

The computer-generated image at right combines data from a seismic survey with data gained by installing sensors inside four oil wells, represented here as squiggly red and yellow diagonals. The colors in the two flat planes and the rippled layer between them measure the relative porosity of the rock masses at this drilling site, with dark purple indicating areas that are most porous and therefore likeliest to contain quantities of oil.

An Experiment in Cosmic Genesis

The large dark area in the picture below is a nebula, a cloud of dust and gas known to astronomers as Barnard 86. The nebula's density obscures what is going on inside — matter-crushing processes of the kind that caused the sun to light up about five billion years ago.

Just as supercomputers help chronicle happenings too small to see, they can unveil processes that dwarf earthly events. One example is the formation of a star, an occurrence that is commonplace in the universe yet is largely hidden from astronomers' view. The birth process is launched when gravity causes an enormous interstellar cloud of dust and gas to start collapsing in on itself. Radio telescopes can observe the em-

bryonic star in this phase, but as the cloud continues to shrink and thicken, it hides the central area for a period of about 100,000 years — until the star becomes hot enough to be detectable by an infrared telescope.

To fathom the secrets of a collapsing cloud, astronomers create mathematical models that describe the interplay of heat, motion, gravity and other factors. For a single simula-

tion, the computer has to perform something on the order of a trillion calculations. Researchers can give their computerized clouds different shapes, or adjust the equation so that the clouds rotate rapidly, slowly, or not at all. Playing out such exercises has suggested why some clouds yield gravitationally linked twins called binary stars, while others collapse into solo stars like our own sun.

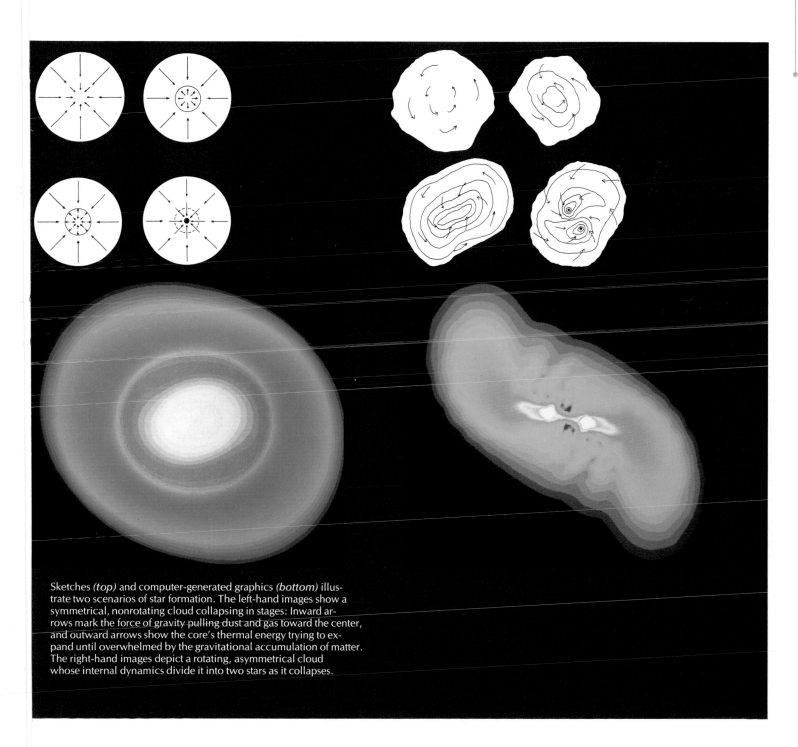

Sketches *(top)* and computer-generated graphics *(bottom)* illustrate two scenarios of star formation. The left-hand images show a symmetrical, nonrotating cloud collapsing in stages: Inward arrows mark the force of gravity pulling dust and gas toward the center, and outward arrows show the core's thermal energy trying to expand until overwhelmed by the gravitational accumulation of matter. The right-hand images depict a rotating, asymmetrical cloud whose internal dynamics divide it into two stars as it collapses.

the Star-100, programs that took full advantage of the machine's vector capabilities ran much faster than similar programs on the scalar 7600. Nonetheless, the Star's performance on the whole was a disappointment. Few problems lend themselves readily — or completely — to vector processing. So a computer with vector capability must also operate as a conventional scalar machine; as a program is run, the computer in effect switches back and forth between scalar and vector mode, depending on the type of computation it is performing.

For the engineers who designed the computer, and especially for its pioneering users, the dual mode was almost more trouble than it was worth. The job of writing programs that could efficiently compartmentalize material into vector and scalar sections proved to be a major stumbling block to exploiting the Star's full potential. In addition, the computer's mechanism for switching between modes ate up so much time that unless the vectors were at least several hundred numbers long, little significant time was saved. And in any case, when the Star had to operate in scalar mode, it was no speedier than its predecessors.

Above and beyond these problems was the Star's susceptibility to a host of mechanical difficulties. For example, its intricate circuits were extremely vulnerable to fluctuations in power and temperature, making it much less reliable than other machines on the market. In the end, few customers were willing to spend some $10 million for the machine. After pouring $75 million into building the Star, Control Data could sell only three.

A machine with similar architecture, Texas Instruments' Advanced Scientific Computer, or ASC, fared no better in the marketplace. Like the Star-100, the ASC was a pipelined vector processor, and it too encountered serious programming and reliability problems. After spending six years to design and build seven ASCs, Texas Instruments also managed to sell only three.

A RADICAL DEPARTURE
The Burroughs machine, the third member of this trio of experiments in computer architecture, was called the ILLIAC IV. It was designed at the University of Illinois, an institution that, since the end of World War II, had gained a lustrous reputation for computer research. The ILLIAC IV (for Illinois Automatic Computer) was built between 1965 and 1971, as a project designed to explore parallelism through the use of a large number of processing units. In a radical departure from von Neumann architecture, it boasted 64 processors, each equipped with its own memory and all intended to operate simultaneously on a single problem. The ILLIAC IV was acknowledged to be the fastest computer of its day—five times speedier than the 7600. Installed in 1972 at Ames Research Laboratory of the National Aeronautics and Space Administration (NASA), it tackled some of the largest aerodynamic problems ever programmed. But like the Star and the ASC, it was plagued by technical difficulties. Also, its unique architecture, which called for carefully dividing computations among the multiple processors, caused so many programming headaches that even its handlers at Ames were hard pressed to conceive of ways to summon its speed. A final count against it was its cost: a sky-high $40 million. Though widely admired by computer engineers, ILLIAC IV was clearly an idea ahead of its time, and it remained a one-of-a-kind curiosity. The Ames researchers finally shut it down in 1981.

By the mid-1970s, Control Data's earlier decision to de-emphasize supercom-

Supercooling for Supercomputers

Perhaps the toughest engineering challenge in the quest to build faster computers is finding ways to keep heat buildup from turning multimillion-dollar machines into useless boxes of melted electronics. Integrated circuits — semiconductor chips made up of thousands of components with switching times of a few billionths of a second (page 107) — enable hardware designers to dramatically increase the speed of a computer's operations by reducing the distance that its electronic signals must travel. But a chip less than an inch square can generate five watts of energy in the form of heat; in densely packed machines, the heat buildup can exceed 100 kilowatts — enough to cause components to fail early and often.

When air cooling proved inadequate, engineers turned to a method similar to that used in household refrigerators. This technique works well enough for most mainframes. It also works for supercomputers such as Control Data Corporation's 6600 (below) and the Cray-1 (overleaf). But for the even faster Cray-2 (page 37), more resourceful solutions — drawing on innovative methods of heat transfer — are required.

As shown in this simplified diagram, the cooling system of the CDC 6600 pumps pressurized liquid Freon from the condenser through coils in the computer's chassis. The Freon draws heat from the computer and evaporates into a gas before returning to the compressor to be repressurized. Reaching temperatures of 110° F., the gas is then channeled to the condenser. Cooled by water circulating in pipes, the Freon gives up its heat and turns back into a liquid.

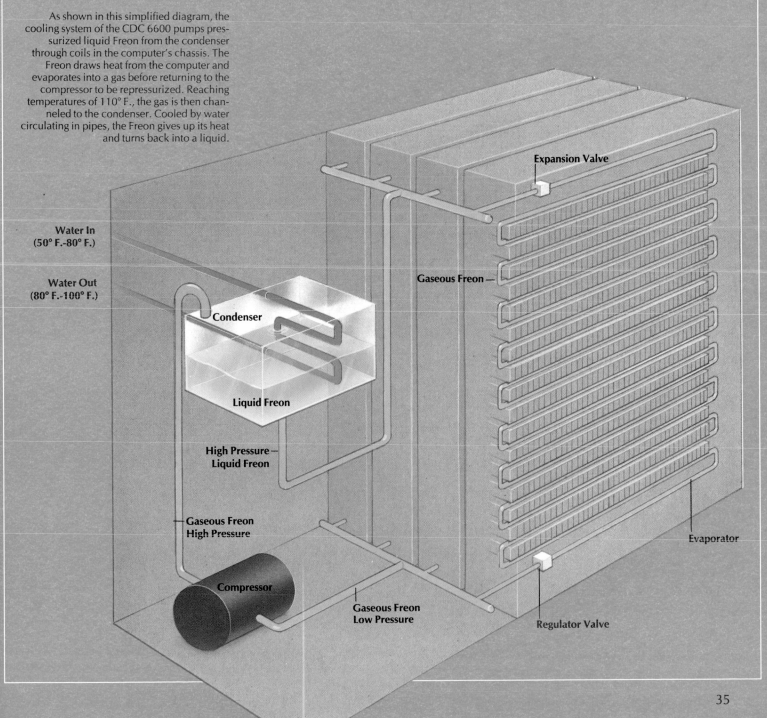

Water In (50° F.-80° F.)

Water Out (80° F.-100° F.)

Condenser

Liquid Freon

High Pressure Liquid Freon

Gaseous Freon High Pressure

Compressor

Gaseous Freon Low Pressure

Expansion Valve

Gaseous Freon —

Evaporator

Regulator Valve

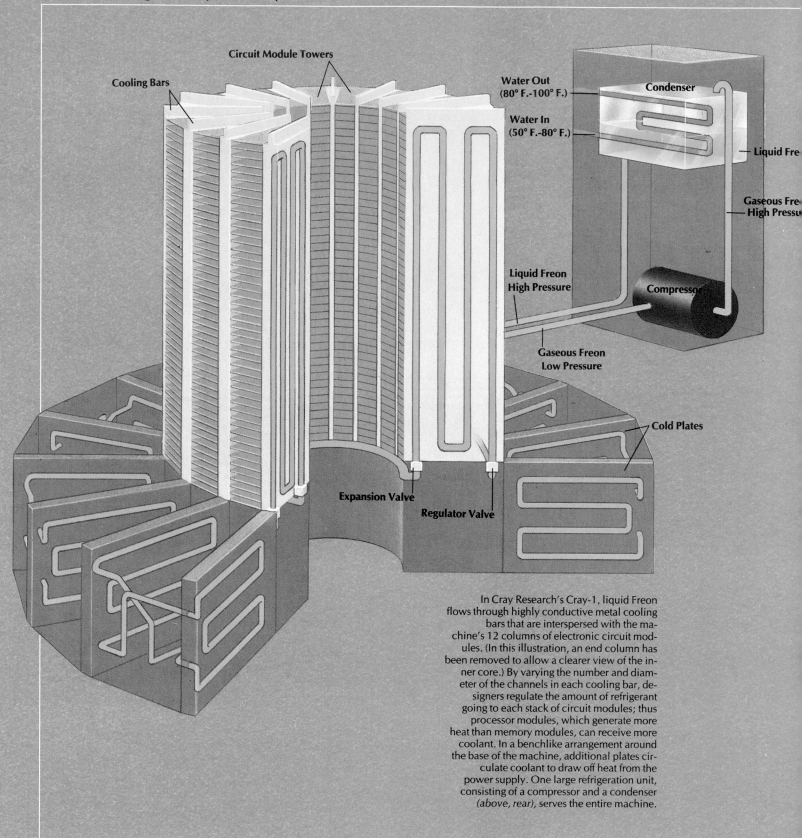

Cooling Bars

Circuit Module Towers

Water Out (80° F.-100° F.)

Condenser

Water In (50° F.-80° F.)

Liquid Fre

Gaseous Fre High Pressu

Liquid Freon High Pressure

Compressor

Gaseous Freon Low Pressure

Cold Plates

Expansion Valve

Regulator Valve

In Cray Research's Cray-1, liquid Freon flows through highly conductive metal cooling bars that are interspersed with the machine's 12 columns of electronic circuit modules. (In this illustration, an end column has been removed to allow a clearer view of the inner core.) By varying the number and diameter of the channels in each cooling bar, designers regulate the amount of refrigerant going to each stack of circuit modules; thus processor modules, which generate more heat than memory modules, can receive more coolant. In a benchlike arrangement around the base of the machine, additional plates circulate coolant to draw off heat from the power supply. One large refrigeration unit, consisting of a compressor and a condenser (*above, rear*), serves the entire machine.

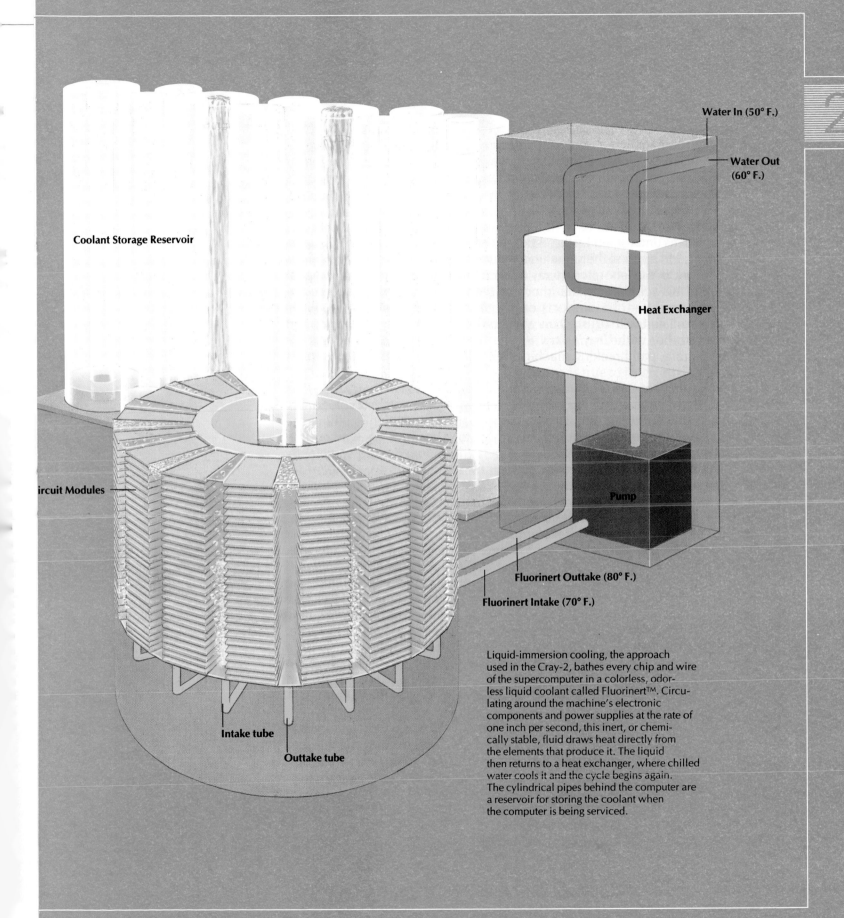

Coolant Storage Reservoir

Water In (50° F.)

Water Out (60° F.)

Heat Exchanger

Circuit Modules

Pump

Fluorinert Outtake (80° F.)

Fluorinert Intake (70° F.)

Intake tube

Outtake tube

Liquid-immersion cooling, the approach used in the Cray-2, bathes every chip and wire of the supercomputer in a colorless, odorless liquid coolant called Fluorinert™. Circulating around the machine's electronic components and power supplies at the rate of one inch per second, this inert, or chemically stable, fluid draws heat directly from the elements that produce it. The liquid then returns to a heat exchanger, where chilled water cools it and the cycle begins again. The cylindrical pipes behind the computer are a reservoir for storing the coolant when the computer is being serviced.

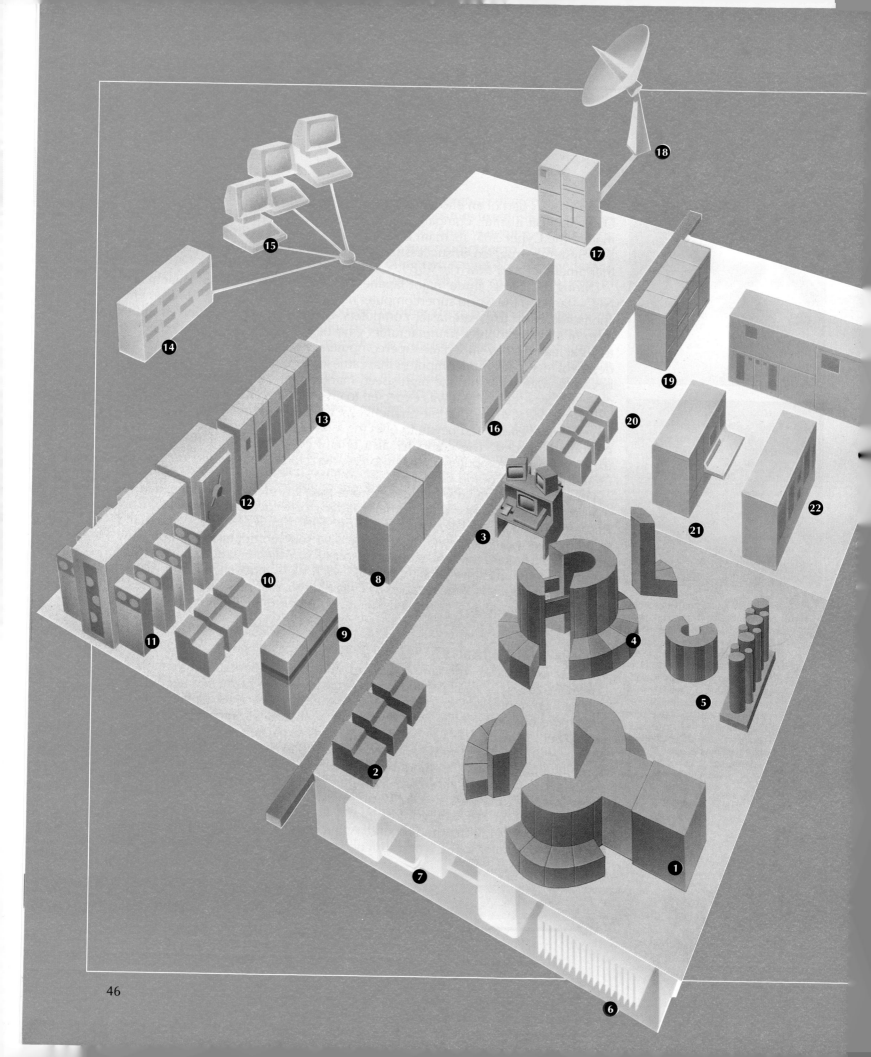

A Computational Powerhouse

A Hardware Roster

COMPUTER ROOM

1. **Cray Y-MP/8/32,** with **input/output processor,** performs an average of 120 megaflops.
2. **Local high-speed disk drives** expand immediate storage capabilities of supercomputers.
3. **Operator console area** lets users monitor work.
4. **X-MP/48,** with **input/output processor,** performs an average of 53 megaflops.
5. **Cray-2,** with coolant storage reservoir, has an operational range of 2 to 133 megaflops.

EQUIPMENT ROOM

6. **Transformers** supply power to supercomputers.
7. **Heat exchangers** cool computer components.

STORAGE AREA

8. **MASS (Multi-Access Storage System) concentrator** buffers data for cartridge storage.
9. **File transport concentrator** buffers incoming data and keeps track of files in storage.
10. **Staging disks** hold data headed for archival storage and can retrieve files in a fraction of a second.
11. **Archival storage library** keeps data on magnetic-tape reels; retrieval time is about two minutes.
12. **Tape vault** provides added shelf storage for reels.
13. **Cartridge library** stores data on cylinders of magnetic tape and retrieves files in several seconds.

REMOTE ACCESS AREA

14. **Local support processor** helps prepare programs.
15. **Local area network** users gain access from workstations.
16. **Gateway computer** clears network communications.
17. **Satellite communications concentrator** speed-matches satellite data.
18. **Satellite dish** connects distant users.

OUTPUT RECORDING AREA

19. **Output file concentrator** buffers high-speed data.
20. **Staging disks** briefly store files for printing.
21. **Microfilm/fiche recorder** can produce hundreds of pages of graphic or printed results per minute.
22. **Strip-film recorder** creates color films of computer-generated simulations.
23. **High-speed laser printer** (18,000 lines per minute).

To make optimum use of the tremendous problem-solving power of supercomputers calls for an equally potent array of support services and peripheral devices. Increasingly, scientists and engineers are sharing supercomputing resources through centers that consolidate the support for several machines. Although configurations vary, the simplified example at left reflects the kinds of equipment — lesser computers, storage units, input/output devices and communications systems — needed to exploit the potential of such a center's great calculating engines.

With advances in satellite and network communications, up to 4,500 users — as many as 2,000 of them at once — can gain access to a center from desk-top terminals in nearby offices and from locations scattered across the country. Some programming is done within the center itself, but the point of entry for remote users is the access area (green), where a gateway computer performs security checks and protocol matching — a technique to ensure that programs developed externally are recognizable to the center's computers. Once accepted, program data travels over an internal communications channel (orange), a very high speed data bus that links all the center's operations. The bus transmits data to the heart of the system, the computer room (red). Here, the supercomputers work their magic, while cooling and power-supply systems in a nearby equipment room (light blue) keep them running at peak efficiency.

Facilities for holding the vast amounts of data supercomputers process and generate are as essential as the computers themselves. The storage area (blue) organizes its capacity — in some cases as much as 13 trillion bits — into a hierarchy of storage levels, from readily accessible staging disks to intermediate tape cartridges and long-term magnetic-tape libraries. Because storage equipment cannot keep pace with the supercomputers, data must be processed through concentrators — computers that buffer data, passing it to the various storage devices at speeds they can handle. Concentrators perform this vital speed-matching in other parts of the system as well, correlating data rates for satellite transmissions and for recording devices in the output-recording area (yellow).

Supercomputer centers work around the clock. Typically, daytime hours are used for analyzing results and for developing programs, which are then run at night and on weekends. Even when these production runs spill over into the day, a center's array of powerful machines can keep work going on other projects.

Livermore Laboratory—which nicknamed it "Bubbles"—than the 60-year-old genius began plotting the Cray-3—a machine that would contain 16 processing units as well as microchips made from gallium arsenide *(pages 112-113),* and that would be no bigger than a breadbox.

With the Cray-3 still a gleam in its designer's eye, the next Cray Research computer on the horizon was the Cray Y-MP, an eight-processor system under development by Steve Chen's team and based on the X-MP. But in late 1987, before the first Y-MP could be completed, Chen quit Cray Research. Once considered the leading candidate to succeed Seymour Cray, he had become frustrated with the company's lack of interest in his next project, an ambitious 64-processor design known as the MP. Within weeks of departing, Chen formed his own company, Supercomputer Systems, Inc. (SSI). The venture was financed in large measure by IBM, which sought to buy an entrée to the supercomputer arena after abandoning it twenty years earlier.

Cray Research completed the Y-MP without Chen and introduced it to customer acclaim in 1988. The company now seemed committed to two independent product lines. One, based on Seymour Cray's work, consisted of a diverse group of machines: the Cray-1, the Cray-2 and the planned Cray-3. The other, inspired by Chen's designs, was an evolutionary sequence that included the X-MP, the Y-MP and the proposed C-90, a 16-processor supercomputer intended to press the limits of silicon technology. Establishing two design groups enabled the company to introduce new machines more often—but at the cost of doubling its already high rate of expenditure for research and development. Revenues could not keep pace.

In May 1989, the company escaped that financial trap with a surprise announcement that made national front-page news. Overburdened by research costs, Cray Research was splitting to form two competing firms. The larger company, which kept the name Cray Research, would remain in Chippewa Falls under chairman John Rollwagen, marketing the X-MP, the Cray-2 and the Y-MP while continuing the C-90 project. It would keep most of the corporate assets—with the key exception of Seymour Cray. Cray himself would move to Colorado Springs and start up Cray Computers, which would begin producing the Cray-3 in the early 1990s. Cray Computers would also build the Cray-4, an advanced version of the Cray-3 intended to reach the marketplace by the year 2000.

To many industry observers, the split followed a familiar pattern. Just as Seymour Cray had left ERA Systems in 1957 and Control Data in 1972, he was resigning once again in search of the breathing room needed to develop his revolutionary machines. In effect, Cray had turned his back on the Cray-2—just as he had abandoned its predecessors. But each of his machines has far outlived its creator's interest and exceeded his expectations. From the CDC 6600 to the Cray-2, his computers have proved to be much more than high-tech adding machines. Because of their capacity for handling data, models of the ocean or a tornado or an oil field could be made rich in detail, more akin to portraits than to stick figures. Just as the advent of the automobile transformed the world's landscapes, the elevator changed city skylines and the air conditioner gave new life to the South, supercomputers have changed the face of modern research and manufacturing. They have become the heavy machinery of the information age, the essential tools for extending the frontiers of human knowledge.

Once embarked on a new supercomputer design, Seymour Cray *(above)* retained little affection for the preceding one, a trait that also governed a favorite hobby—boatbuilding. Every winter for many years, Cray built a wooden sailboat, sailed it the following summer, then made a bonfire of it in the fall so that it wouldn't distract him as he planned the next one.

Beating Hardware Bottlenecks

At the heart of a high-speed digital computer is a complex web of circuitry linking millions of switches that combine to manipulate electronically stored information. The organization of these interconnections, called the computer's architecture, is a major factor in determining the machine's operating speed.

Although a number of architectures are possible in theory, one design, outlined by computer pioneer John von Neumann in 1945, dominated the first 40 years of electronic computing. Traditional von Neumann architecture *(pages 50-51)* is characterized by three elements: a memory where instructions and data are stored; a central processing unit (CPU) where instructions are interpreted and data is processed; and a communication channel, or bus, that connects the two.

Many extremely fast computers have been built in accordance with the von Neumann principles, but ultimately this architecture limits the speed of computation by imposing a sequential mode of operation. Instructions flow from memory into the CPU one at a time, and the CPU must finish the work dictated by one instruction before it can turn to another. Even a simple operation, such as adding A to B and storing the result at C, involves a dozen separate steps *(pages 52-53)*. Repeating these steps one at a time for a million data values — common in aeronautical or atmospheric research, for example — takes the computer perhaps a tenth of a second. Hardly noticeable to a human, this is a substantial stretch of time for a machine that operates in billionths of a second. And the fractions of seconds can quickly increase to minutes or hours in large problems where such sequential calculations are repeated over and over.

One approach to the problem is a design principle called concurrency, or parallelism — making different parts of the computer labor simultaneously on separate segments of the problem. Concurrency can be implemented on many levels. For example, the CPU can be subdivided and set to work on different stages of successive instructions, or the slowness of one element may be offset by adding identical elements to share the work. Parallel operation, which can extend even to multiple processors *(pages 62-65)*, marks a fundamental shift from von Neumann architecture. A given supercomputer usually employs several of these speed-enhancing features; for clarity, each of the machines illustrated on the following pages incorporates only one improvement.

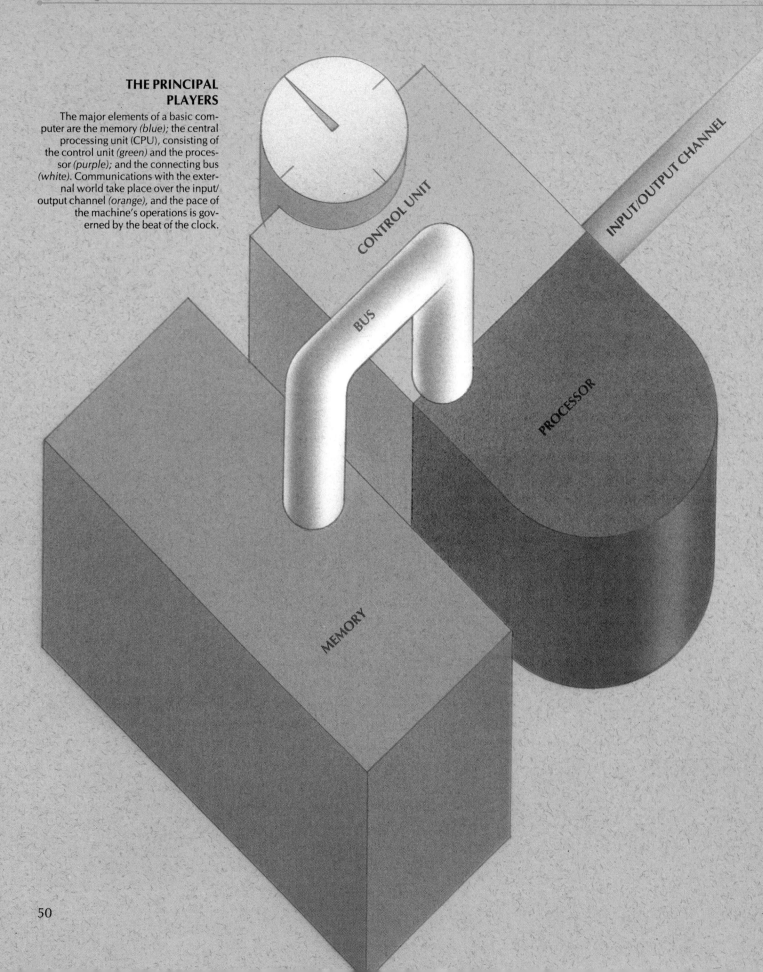

THE PRINCIPAL PLAYERS

The major elements of a basic computer are the memory *(blue);* the central processing unit (CPU), consisting of the control unit *(green)* and the processor *(purple);* and the connecting bus *(white).* Communications with the external world take place over the input/output channel *(orange),* and the pace of the machine's operations is governed by the beat of the clock.

CONTROL UNIT

INPUT/OUTPUT CHANNEL

BUS

PROCESSOR

MEMORY

Anatomy of a Serial Machine

The organization of the main elements in a conventional von Neumann computer is schematically shown at left. Programs and the data to be processed are stored in the computer's memory, which is connected to the two-part central processing unit (CPU) by a pathway called the bus. Each piece of information is assigned to a memory location that has a unique numerical address, allowing the information to be retrieved by the CPU when needed.

The actual work of a computer is carried out in the CPU, where the processor performs arithmetic and logical operations on data that has been transferred from memory. The control unit directs the flow of instructions and data to and from memory. It also directs information through the input/output channel to and from external devices, including monitors, printers and plotters, and information storage media such as magnetic tape. As described below, the von Neumann design for carrying out each of these control-unit functions can result in significant operational slowdowns. One of the most significant hindrances to speed in a conventional computer is the sequential way it carries out its work. Traditional programs are made up of hundreds or thousands of instructions, which are executed one at a time. Each instruction — for performing logical comparisons, simple addition or more complex mathematical functions — triggers a specific set of operations that in turn must be executed in step-by-step fashion. But much of the computer's internal activity is the same for every instruction: Again and again, the various elements of the machine perform their specialized tasks in a complex electronic minuet called the instruction cycle.

The computer represented schematically on the next two pages has a cycle that loops through four steps (cycles of many more steps are common): The control unit fetches a program instruction from memory, decodes it and orders the transfer of data from memory to the processor; the processor then performs the desired operation on the data. Each instruction must progress through this cycle before the control unit can fetch another one. At any given phase of the cycle, some elements of the computer are idle. Thus, much of the effort to speed up computers is aimed at finding ways to get around the inefficiency of sequential operations.

A Gallery of Speed Thieves

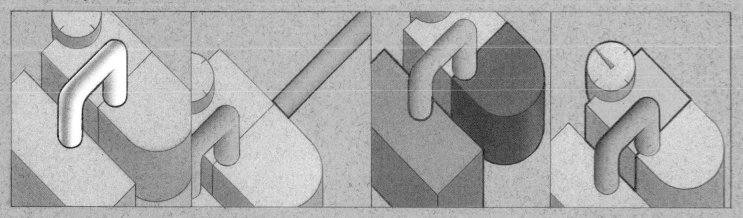

The bus

A single bus between memory and the CPU can carry only one control signal or one piece of information at a time, and in only one direction at a time. Thus, the CPU is idle while instructions or data are transferred over from the memory and when results are returned there.

Input and output

When the instructions and data of a problem require more space than is available in memory, they must be held in long-term storage devices. During the running of a program, the CPU often must stop its processing to supervise the steps needed to bring the information from external storage into memory and to send results back out to external storage if necessary.

Memory

The more capacious a computer's memory, the less frequently data and instructions must be brought in from external storage. Given the amount of memory needed for modern computing, designers usually employ cheaper — and slower — electronic switches in memory than are used for the processor. This speed mismatch means that the CPU must often stop to await the arrival of a piece of information.

The clock

A computer's clock, like a metronome, maintains a beat that regulates the work of all the elements. It is set to allow enough time between each tick for a signal to travel the longest path within the CPU. Crowding a computer's electronic components closer together can thus allow the designer to speed up the clock. But this often requires the addition of expensive cooling systems to prevent heat build-up.

A Serial Computer's Work Pattern

Executing a LOAD Instruction

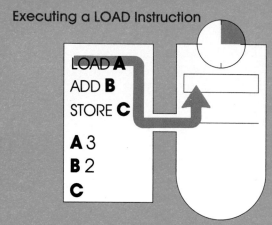

Fetch instruction. In the first phase of this computer's four-part cycle, the control unit reads the information stored at a particular address in memory and brings the program instruction located there — in this case, LOAD A — into the CPU.

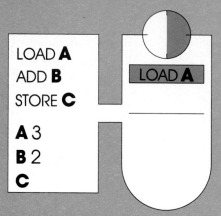

Decode. In the second phase, the control unit translates the instruction: It separates the opcode (LOAD), which identifies the operation to be performed, from the operand (A), which names the memory address of the piece of data that is to be operated upon.

Executing an ADD Instruction

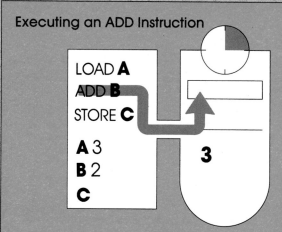

Fetch instruction. In the first phase of the next instruction cycle, the control unit reads the information stored at the succeeding address in memory and brings the program instruction into the CPU.

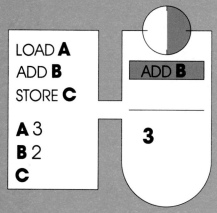

Decode. The control unit again breaks down the instruction into its components. The opcode ADD tells the control unit to bring the value stored at the address identified by the operand B into the processor and add it to the value already there.

Executing a STORE Instruction

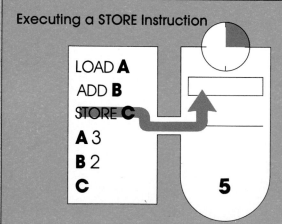

Fetch instruction. As before, the control unit reads the information stored at the next address in memory — STORE C — and brings the instruction into the central processing unit.

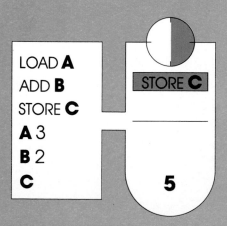

Decode. Broken into the opcode STORE and the operand C, the instruction directs the control unit to identify the result of the addition — 5 — as C and then to transfer it into memory.

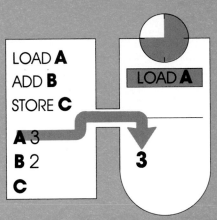

Data transfer. Carrying out the action required by the LOAD opcode, the control unit directs the memory to transmit the data located at the address identified as A. This value — 3 — is put in a small, high-speed storage unit within the CPU called a register.

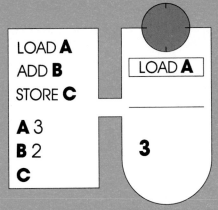

Process. In the final phase of the cycle for this instruction, the processor remains idle because all the actions triggered by the LOAD opcode have been performed.

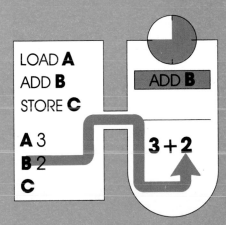

Data transfer. The control unit directs memory to transfer the piece of data at B — in this case, the value 2 — into another register in the processor. Now both numbers to be added are present in the CPU.

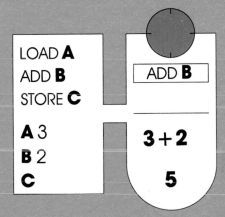

Process. In this phase of the instruction cycle, the processor performs the actual arithmetic operation, adding 3 and 2. The resulting value, 5, is temporarily held in the processor.

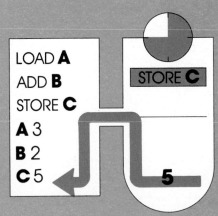

Data transfer. The control unit reverses the direction of data transfer, sending the value 5 to memory, where it is stored in the location indicated by its name, C.

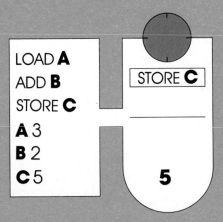

Process. The processor again remains idle in the final phase, having executed all the operations required by the opcode STORE.

Striking a Balance among the Components

To overcome some of the delays inherent in one-step-at-a-time von Neumann machines, designers have investigated a number of ways to get the computer to perform several operations simultaneously. One of the first innovations devised was to add an input/output (I/O) processor *(below)*, a separate computer dedicated entirely to communication with the outside world. The I/O processor relieves the CPU of overseeing the movement of information to and from the mechanical devices used for printing and storing information, which may be as much as a thousand times slower than the all-electronic central processor.

Other design changes aim at reducing the speed imbalance between processor and memory that often keeps the processor waiting for data. Partitioning the memory into several smaller units, or banks, for instance, allows the banks to function concurrently but out of phase with one another and thus keep data streaming to the processor. For example, if fetching an item from memory takes four times as long as processing it in the CPU, four banks taking turns can keep the central processor constantly supplied with information at its peak speed.

Another approach to balancing the performance of processor and memory is to insert a small, fast memory unit, called a cache, that temporarily holds data in transit between the CPU and main memory. Because data can be retrieved much more quickly from the small cache than from the larger main memory, the processor is less often required to wait for its working materials.

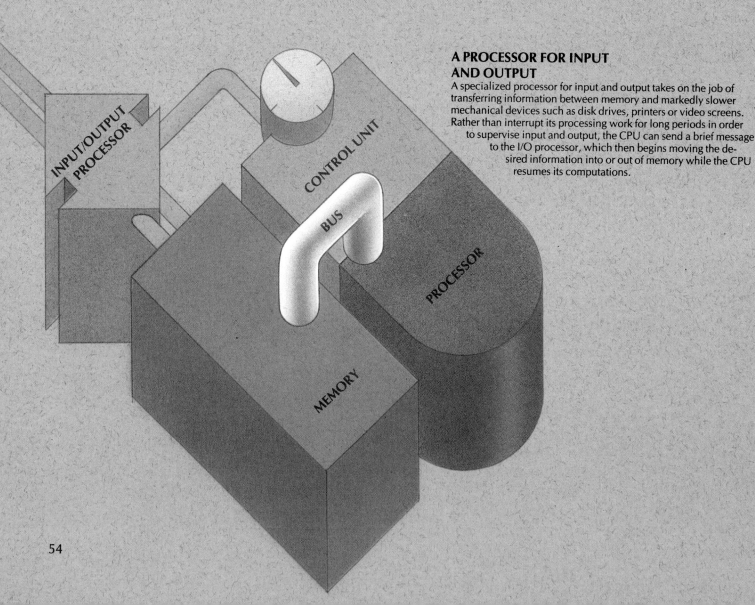

A PROCESSOR FOR INPUT AND OUTPUT

A specialized processor for input and output takes on the job of transferring information between memory and markedly slower mechanical devices such as disk drives, printers or video screens. Rather than interrupt its processing work for long periods in order to supervise input and output, the CPU can send a brief message to the I/O processor, which then begins moving the desired information into or out of memory while the CPU resumes its computations.

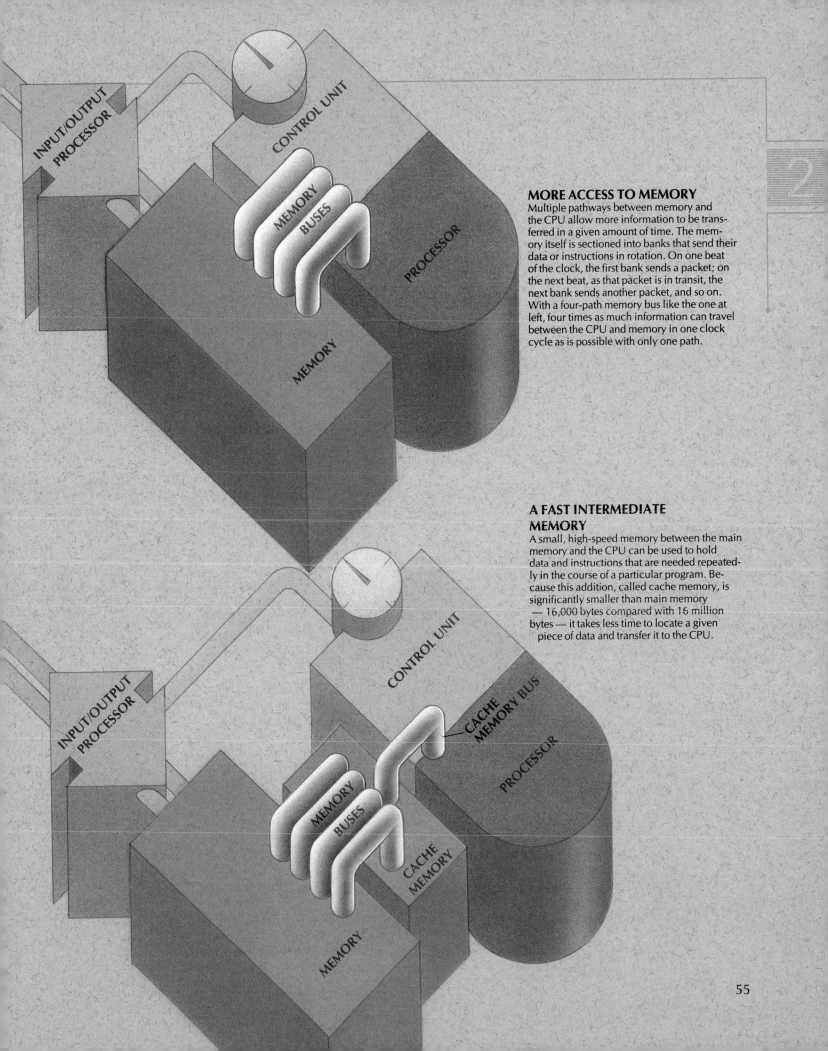

MORE ACCESS TO MEMORY

Multiple pathways between memory and the CPU allow more information to be transferred in a given amount of time. The memory itself is sectioned into banks that send their data or instructions in rotation. On one beat of the clock, the first bank sends a packet; on the next beat, as that packet is in transit, the next bank sends another packet, and so on. With a four-path memory bus like the one at left, four times as much information can travel between the CPU and memory in one clock cycle as is possible with only one path.

A FAST INTERMEDIATE MEMORY

A small, high-speed memory between the main memory and the CPU can be used to hold data and instructions that are needed repeatedly in the course of a particular program. Because this addition, called cache memory, is significantly smaller than main memory — 16,000 bytes compared with 16 million bytes — it takes less time to locate a given piece of data and transfer it to the CPU.

INPUT/OUTPUT PROCESSOR

CONTROL UNIT

MEMORY BUSES

PROCESSOR

MEMORY

INPUT/OUTPUT PROCESSOR

CONTROL UNIT

CACHE MEMORY BUS

PROCESSOR

MEMORY BUSES

CACHE MEMORY

MEMORY

55

Special Assistants
to the Processor

Computers working on complex mathematical problems can be made faster by tailoring the CPU for number-crunching. The simplest way to do this is by dividing the CPU in two, completely separating the control unit from the processor, and then adding specialized circuits to the processor to help with the mathematical work. These helper circuits are designed to do only a few tasks, but to do them very quickly.

In one alternative architecture *(below)*, the processor is partitioned into elements called functional units, each capable of a particular kind of calculation — addition, for instance, or multiplication. If a given computation involves several kinds of calculations, as is true in most programs, they can be performed concurrently in the different units; for example, one or more additions might take place at the

BREAKING THE JOB DOWN

The processor in this simplified computer is split into several functional units, each designed to provide optimal performance for a small set of arithmetic operations. This processor has units for addition and subtraction, multiplication and division; real computers used for complex mathematical problems might have many more units for such specialized operations as adding large arrays of numbers. The control unit directs operations in memory with signals carried by the green channel and receives instructions through the red channel. As each instruction is decoded, it is routed to the proper functional unit for execution; data for the operation comes directly from memory to the processor through the purple channel.

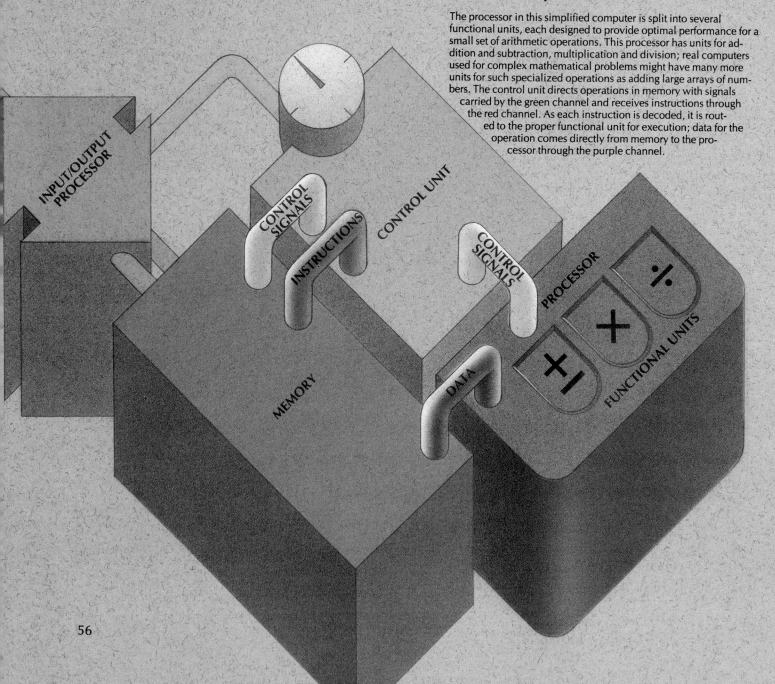

same time as a multiplication. A drawback to this division-of-labor scheme is that some units may be able to perform a single operation faster than others: One addition, for example, takes less time than one multiplication. To avoid errors caused by intermediate results being used out of sequence, the program must be designed to coordinate the actions of the functional units.

Another way to specialize the processing is to link a mathematical coprocessor to the main processor. The coprocessor is organized to perform some functions — typically, floating-point arithmetic (page 40) — much faster than the main processor. Unlike a functional unit, which is run by the control unit, a coprocessor is subordinate to the main processor, which simply hands off data and instructions.

SPLITTING OFF THE HARD PARTS

Here a computer's processor is augmented by a specialized assistant called a coprocessor, which handles a narrow range of tasks. The coprocessor is designed to perform its operations — such as floating-point addition or binary logic — with great speed. The coprocessor receives data and instructions from the main processing unit and passes its results back to the main processor, where they may be used in further computations or sent to memory.

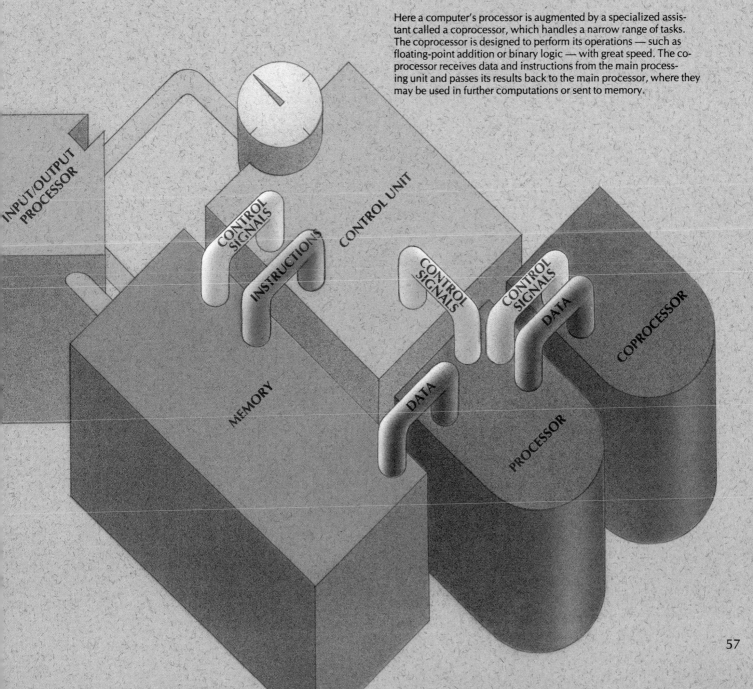

Making Use of Idle Time

As demonstrated on pages 52-53, the CPU in a conventional computer executes a single instruction in each instruction cycle, moving sequentially through the phases of the cycle before beginning the next instruction. Because each phase is handled by a different element in the control unit, this approach means that at any given point in the cycle, parts of the control unit are idle. A design concept called pipelining speeds up the computer by putting these idle elements to work and allowing the CPU to operate on more than one instruction at a time.

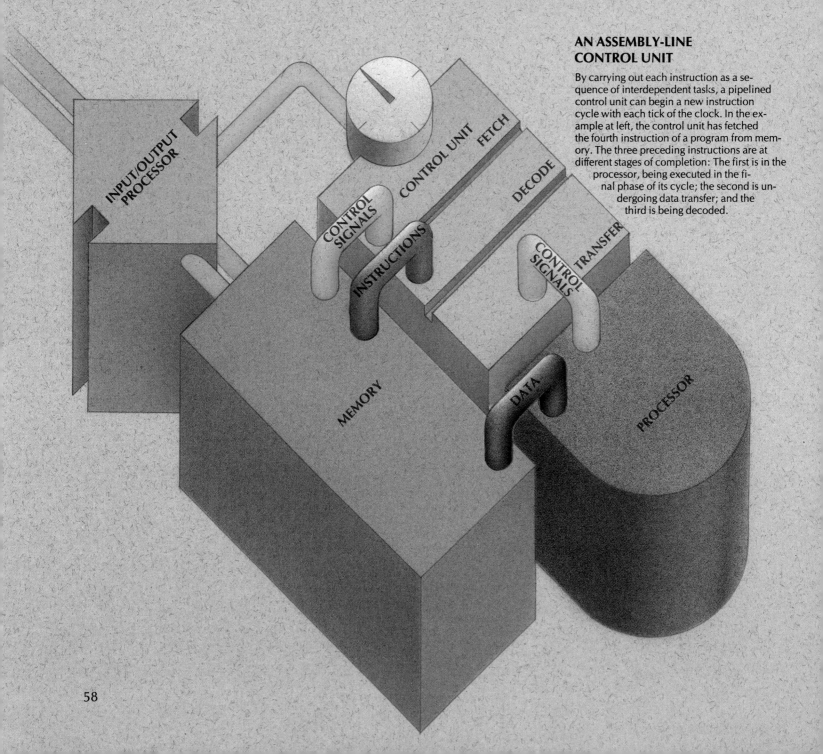

AN ASSEMBLY-LINE CONTROL UNIT

By carrying out each instruction as a sequence of interdependent tasks, a pipelined control unit can begin a new instruction cycle with each tick of the clock. In the example at left, the control unit has fetched the fourth instruction of a program from memory. The three preceding instructions are at different stages of completion: The first is in the processor, being executed in the final phase of its cycle; the second is undergoing data transfer; and the third is being decoded.

In a pipelined control unit, the separate elements are organized to function in assembly-line fashion. On every tick of the clock, a new instruction moves into the first station, while each subsequent station completes its subtask — decoding the instruction, for example — and passes the result to the next station. By the end of four clock ticks, a central processing unit with a four-phase instruction cycle (below) will have executed the first instruction and filled the pipeline with instructions in varying stages of completion; an instruction is then executed on each succeeding tick of the clock, rather than on every fourth tick, as in a conventional von Neumann computer.

The principles of pipelining can also be applied to the processor that actually executes each instruction (box), and in designs far more complex than those shown here. For example, in a processor with separate functional units (page 56), each unit may be pipelined; the same methods can be used with a mathematics coprocessor.

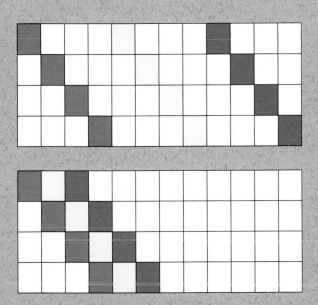

THE EFFICIENCY OF PIPELINING

The chart at left compares the performance of an ordinary central processing unit with that of one that has been pipelined, each employing a four-phase instruction cycle to carry out a simple routine consisting of three instructions. The ordinary CPU (top) must complete an entire cycle of four clock ticks before it can begin the next instruction; three instructions thus require 12 clock ticks to complete. In a pipelined CPU (bottom), which starts on a new instruction with each tick, the same task is completed in half the time.

Pipelines in the Processor

For simple mathematical operations such as addition, the final, or execute, phase of the instruction cycle takes only one clock tick; complex operations, such as floating-point multiplication, take much longer. To reduce the processing time for problems with many complex operations, the processor can be pipelined in the same way as the control unit. In the four-pipe processor at right, the fourth step of a floating-point addition is being carried out while the earlier stages of processing on succeeding operands are performed in other parts of the pipeline.

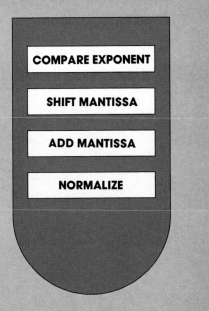

COMPARE EXPONENT

SHIFT MANTISSA

ADD MANTISSA

NORMALIZE

The Vector Approach

One of the most successful architectural approaches to speeding up a von Neumann computer is the addition of a processor that is designed to manipulate specially created lists of numbers called vectors. The processor treats each vector as a single entity; it executes an instruction by performing the same operation on every number in the vector simultaneously. In arithmetic operations such as addition or multiplication, for example, the numbers of one vector are paired for manipulation with numbers in another vector of equal length *(below, right)*. Adding two vectors together

SPECIAL TREATMENT FOR VECTORS

Unlike a coprocessor, which is subordinate to the main processor *(page 57)*, a vector processor receives instructions directly from the control unit. It works only on vectors — long strings of numbers — by processing all the values in the vector simultaneously. In the schematic computer shown here, each vector can contain four values; when a computation is completed, the result is also a vector with four values. A vector computer retains an ordinary scalar processor to perform calculations on numbers that are not part of a vector; each processor transfers information to and from memory along its own pathway.

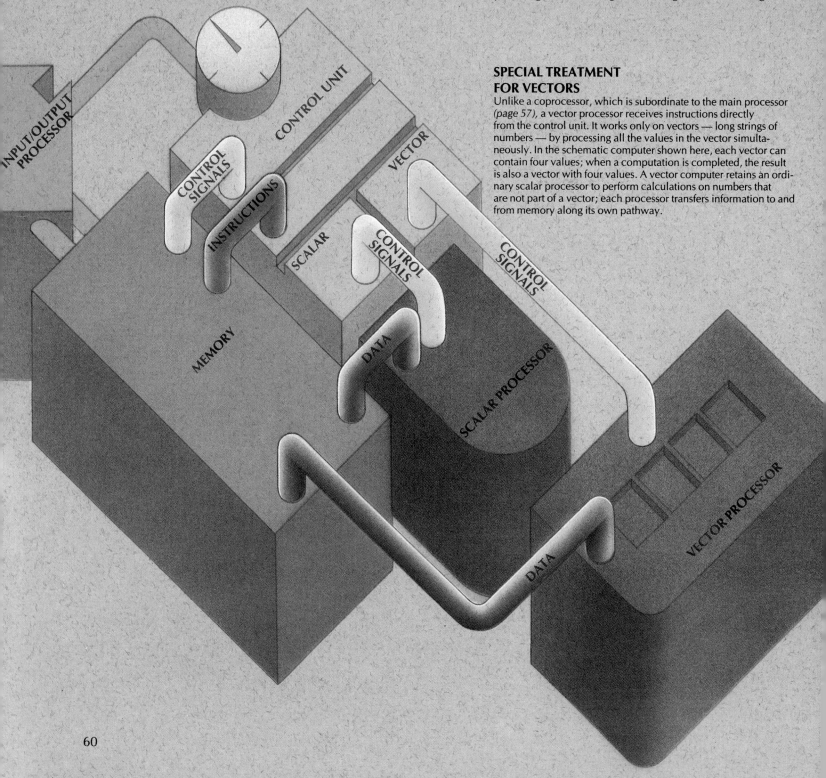

thus takes only as long as it takes to add two numbers.

Computers with vector processors are useful in a variety of applications. Most are scientific computations such as molecular modeling or fluid-flow analysis *(pages 20-23)*, which are characterized by a large volume of data that can easily be organized into lists when the program is written. Even in these problems, however, not all the data lends itself to this structure. A vector processor is thus usually coupled with an ordinary, or scalar, processor to handle computations with nonvectorized data.

While the earliest vector processors usually had a fixed vector length of 32 or 64 numbers, machines capable of processing vectors as long as 65,536 numbers have since been developed. And in the most powerful supercomputers, the control unit, scalar processor and vector processor are all pipelined. At its maximum theoretical speed, such a machine can produce a vector result with every tick of the clock.

LOAD A	5
ADD B	7
STORE C	12

LOAD D	1
ADD E	3
STORE F	4

LOAD G	6
ADD H	13
STORE I	19

LOAD J	8
ADD K	14
STORE L	22

LOAD V_1	5	1	6	8
ADD V_2	7	3	13	14
STORE V_3	12	4	19	22

THE BENEFITS OF VECTORS

A vector processor performs the same kinds of mathematical operations that an ordinary scalar processor performs, but it works on many numbers concurrently. In a scalar processor, the three instructions required to add a pair of numbers and store the result must be repeated for each individual addition; the processing of four such pairs *(left)* takes 12 instruction cycles (each composed of four or more phases) to complete. In a vector processor *(above)*, the same four pairs of numbers can be loaded, added and stored as vectors, completing the processing in only three cycles, or one quarter of the time.

An Array of Workers under One Boss

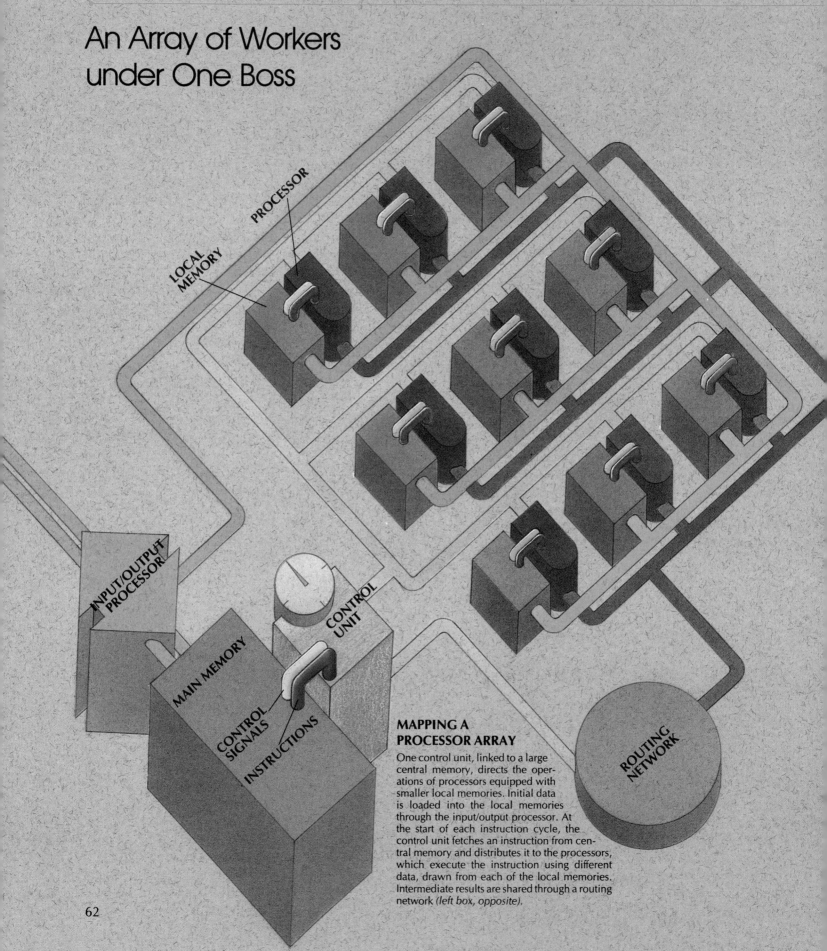

PROCESSOR

LOCAL MEMORY

INPUT/OUTPUT PROCESSOR

MAIN MEMORY

CONTROL UNIT

CONTROL SIGNALS

INSTRUCTIONS

ROUTING NETWORK

MAPPING A PROCESSOR ARRAY

One control unit, linked to a large central memory, directs the operations of processors equipped with smaller local memories. Initial data is loaded into the local memories through the input/output processor. At the start of each instruction cycle, the control unit fetches an instruction from central memory and distributes it to the processors, which execute the instruction using different data, drawn from each of the local memories. Intermediate results are shared through a routing network (left box, opposite).

However fast a vector processor may be, it retains the built-in limitation of being only one unit. To gain speed for large-scale number crunching, one alternative — and a real departure from conventional von Neumann architecture — is a processor array, which places several processors under the direction of a single control unit. Each processor has its own small memory for storing initial data and intermediate results, and the processors can share information with one another through a connecting system called a routing network. At the start of a program, each processor is given data for a small part of the job. The processors work in lockstep, performing identical operations on their separate data. At the completion of the job, the partial results are combined into the final product.

When one processor needs to communicate with another, the routing network functions like a telephone exchange: The calling processor waits for a response before sending or requesting data. Because this waiting can slow the machine's overall speed, processor arrays are best suited to problems with many small parts that can be computed independently. In image processing, for example *(bottom)*, each unit can work with data for a different section of the picture; the values that describe one area of the image are usually not related to the values that describe another area, and little communication is necessary.

Whatever the level of interaction, the speed of the routing network itself affects the computer's overall performance. The fastest network, in theory, is one that allows every processor to communicate directly with every other one. But a machine with hundreds of processors would require costly circuitry and complicated programming. The greater the number of processors, the more important it is to limit the connections to the pattern best tailored to the jobs the computer will run. For many operations used in processing images, for instance, processors need to communicate only with their immediate neighbors.

Processing Numbers Arranged in a Grid

For efficient computing with an array processor, data values are grouped in gridlike structures that correspond to the arrangement of processors in the computer. These arrays of values can then be manipulated as single units. In the example at right, two arrays are added together to produce a result that is also an array of values.

3	15	1
4	21	2
3	1	3

+

6	2	3
15	9	2
6	9	1

=

9	17	4
19	30	4
9	10	4

A Web for Communication

Linking each of nine processors to all the others in an array requires 36 connections; doubling the processors would more than quadruple the links. In large arrays, the control unit can direct a routing network to connect processors only as necessary.

Consulting on Image Analysis

Part of an image is divided into a grid, and each processor reports its grid square as red or white. The center processor's data is ambiguous, so it polls its neighbors and votes with the majority, assigning red to its square.

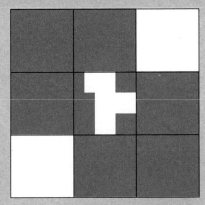

Two Kinds of Multicomputing

Although a processor array speeds program execution by applying more than one processor to the task, it is relatively inflexible because it has only one control unit: At any given moment, all of the processors must execute the same instruction. This limitation can be overcome by supplying each processor with its own control unit, thus enabling the computer to perform different operations simultaneously. Such a machine can, for example, run dissimilar parts of one program concurrently; it can even run more than one program at once, devoting a separate processing element (control unit plus processor) to each.

The two kinds of architecture that incorporate more than one processing element are the multiprocessor, which has a

A Controlling Network

In a computer with multiple, independent processors, a crossbar switching network *(below)* is used to mediate conflicting demands for access to memory and to input/output channels. The switching network is a mesh of intersecting wires; at each junction is a simple processor that has a built-in set of rules for determining which requests are to be given priority.

A MULTIPROCESSOR

Each of the linked elements in a multiprocessor is, in effect, an entire CPU, with a processor and a control unit. All share a common memory, which is partitioned into separate modules so that different processing elements can have access to memory simultaneously. A routing network *(box, left),* routes input and output, and provides each processing element with direct access to memory and to the other units. In transferring information between processing elements, the sender stores the item in memory and notifies the receiver of the memory address where the item is stored; the receiver then fetches the data from that address.

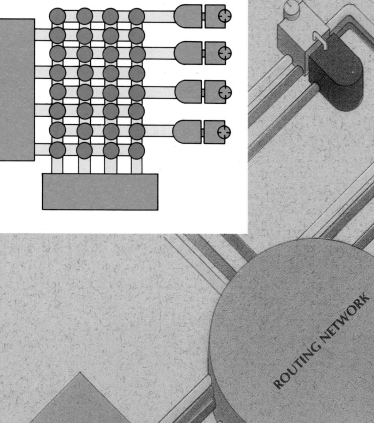

ROUTING NETWORK

PROCESSING ELEMENT

MEMORY

INPUT/OUTPUT PROCESSOR

single large memory unit shared by all of the processing elements, and the multicomputer, in which the central memory is augmented by smaller memory units directly connected to each processing element. Both designs incorporate a routing network that handles communications among the processors as well as between them and memory.

Because the multiprocessor relies on a single shared memory, it needs features that prevent more than one processor at a time from working with data in a particular part of memory. In effect, a processor gets a busy signal if another is fetching the data, using it in computation or returning it to memory. To avoid delays arising from this kind of conflict, the programmer must divide the program appropriately (pages 92-95).

In a multicomputer, the problem of contention for data in memory is largely overcome, since the data that each processor needs is stored in its own individual memory. Delays do occur, however, when one processor requires information that is in midcomputation elsewhere. In that case, the processor must wait for the information to arrive and be stored in its local memory. Again, programmers try to avoid such delays by minimizing the requirement for interprocessor communications.

A MULTICOMPUTER

In a multicomputer, each processing element has its own memory and is effectively a self-sufficient computer. Each computer can work on its part of a problem independently, pausing to exchange data with others as necessary. A routing network connects the computing units with one another, with memory and with the input/output channels. To transfer information from one unit to another, the sender transmits the data to the receiver's memory.

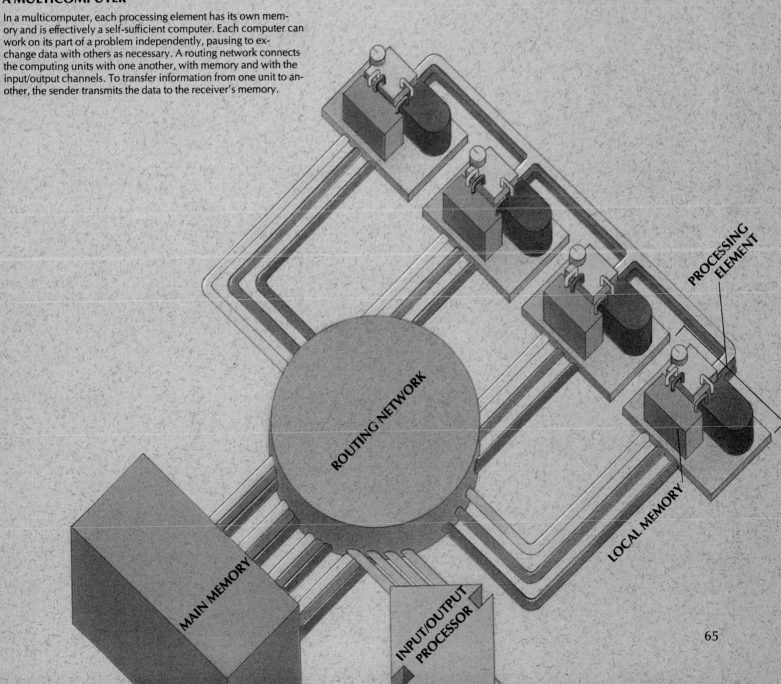

PROCESSING ELEMENT

ROUTING NETWORK

LOCAL MEMORY

MAIN MEMORY

INPUT/OUTPUT PROCESSOR

Alternatives
to Supercomputers

3

It has long been an axiom in computing that speed costs money. Top speed, by this logic, would cost the kind of money usually available only to deep-pocketed corporations or government-funded laboratories. But as it happens, a low budget is not necessarily a sentence to snail-paced computation. Even as they strive for victory in the supercomputer sweepstakes, computer makers have vied to give cost-conscious customers fast machines with relatively low price tags. Some of their entries are general-purpose devices called minicomputers, physically much smaller than supercomputers but capable of doing similar jobs — albeit not as quickly. All things considered, minicomputers often provide more speed per dollar than their larger cousins. Economy is also the hallmark of another class of machine — specialized number-crunching processors that are attached to general-purpose computers. By doing mathematical calculations at a much faster rate than the host computer can attain, these peripheral processors greatly increase the overall speed of a system with only a small rise in price.

Introduced to meet the particular needs of scientists, both types of inexpensive machines have opened up new ways of using computers, bringing enormous power to bear on problems that would once have been beyond solution. Their modest cost can make it practical to devote a computer to a single application — perhaps even to a single user. Adapted to many purposes, in venues as disparate as hospitals and nuclear submarines, they are the basis for some of the greatest corporate success stories in the computer industry.

The era of low-cost computing began in the early 1960s with the introduction of the PDP-1 by Digital Equipment Corporation (DEC). The company was founded on a shoestring in 1957 by former M.I.T. researchers who saw an untapped market for economical computers, particularly in science laboratories. Their judgment proved as good as the machines they built; by the 1980s, DEC was second only to IBM as a manufacturer of computers in the United States.

The force behind DEC was Kenneth Olsen, a soft-spoken engineer whose quiet demeanor masked a tremendous drive and capacity for hard work. Raised in the old tool-and-die center of Stratford, Connecticut, Olsen earned a degree in electrical engineering from M.I.T. and stayed on there to pursue graduate studies in the same subject. In 1950, at 24 years of age, he went to work at the school's Digital Computer Laboratory as a research assistant, joining an exceptional group of young engineers working on the lab's main project, an advanced computer called Whirlwind.

Whirlwind, built under a contract with the U.S. Navy and the U.S. Air Force, was radically different from other computers of the time. In the early 1950s, most computers did their work in batches. Information — both programs and data — was recorded on punched cards that were fed to the computer a job at a time, and results were recorded by a teletype printer. If the printed output indicated that the cards contained an error, the user would have to punch new cards to correct the problem and then go to the end of the line to use the computer again. By contrast, Whirlwind interacted directly with a human operator in "real time" — processing incoming data instantaneously and presenting the results on a video screen for viewing by the operator, who could point a light gun at the screen to indicate an action for the computer to carry out immediately.

One of Whirlwind's major components was its huge magnetic core memory, at the time a new and untried technology consisting of grids of interconnected iron rings. Because it was important to check the memory's reliability before using it, the designers decided to create a smaller computer that could test the magnetic cores in actual use. The task was turned over to Olsen and fellow engineer Harlan Anderson, who built a machine appropriately called the Memory Test Computer, or MTC. One of the first computers intended as a tool for scientific experiments, MTC could produce audio output as well as interact with its users through video screens. The one-of-a-kind computer was soon a favorite of scientists and engineers in the Digital Computer Laboratory.

Whirlwind became the prototype for the computers that would be used in SAGE (Semi-Automatic Ground Environment), a nationwide network for American air defense. The Soviet Union had recently developed long-range bombers capable of penetrating American airspace — a threat against which the existing U.S. air-defense system was hopelessly inadequate. The new system would need to be able to respond in real time to incoming data — in this case, radar signals of enemy bombers. Also crucial was the dependability of the magnetic core memories, in which the SAGE computers would store constantly changing data related to tracking and intercepting targets. Olsen got the job of developing a computer to test new magnetic cores and transistorized circuits like those that were to be used for the SAGE project. Norman Taylor, Olsen's boss, gave him a small staff and a tight deadline: For the project to stay on schedule, the test computer had to be designed and constructed from scratch in the span of just 10 months.

Olsen's first response was that it could not be done, but Taylor knew that his hard-charging engineer would respond to a challenge. "Do it in nine months," Taylor said, "and I'll buy you a case of Scotch." The whisky meant little to teetotaler Olsen, but he rose immediately to the dare that went with it. He and his staff rolled up their sleeves and plunged into the assignment, coming up with a design for a transistorized machine that was dubbed the TX-0. (The designation TX-1 had already been used for a rejected design.) The team worked nights and weekends until the job was done — in time to win the bet.

WORKING WITH IBM

Olsen's achievement with the TX-0 cemented his reputation as an innovative engineer and effective team leader. But as he soon found out, he still had much to learn. The contract to build the SAGE network went to IBM, and M.I.T. sent Olsen to the IBM plant in Poughkeepsie, New York, to supervise production. Immersed in this much larger cooperative effort for more than a year, the engineering whiz got his first hard look at the frustrating world of corporate production. "Olsen was a bona fide engineer," Norman Taylor later recalled. "If something didn't work, he'd take his coat off and redo it himself. The inefficiencies of a large operation like IBM's were appalling to Olsen. But his experience at IBM whetted his appetite for bigger things." As Olsen confided at the time to Taylor: "Norm, I can beat these guys at their own game."

By the time Olsen had completed his work on the SAGE project, he was 31 years old and itching for new mountains to climb. Aware that an academic career of the sort he had experienced as a research scientist at M.I.T. would never satisfy him — "I thought it really wasn't fun unless you influenced the outside world," he said later — he also recognized that he could never be happy in the rigidly structured environment of a large corporation like IBM. Although he rejected a proposal from a group of businessmen to start a company with them, the offer started him thinking about launching an enterprise of his own. Olsen was convinced there was a market — initially in the research community and perhaps later in business — for fast machines, like M.I.T.'s Whirlwind, that allowed direct communication with a user. He foresaw interactive computers as extensions of the user.

Olsen talked M.I.T. colleague Harlan Anderson into joining the venture. Unfazed by their lack of practical knowledge about starting a company, the partners went to the library and read every book they could find on the subject. They poured their savings and those of several associates into the new venture. Then, as the money ran low, the pair turned to American Research & Development (ARD), a venture-capital firm whose specialty was backing embryonic high-tech companies. The firm's president, an imposing retired army air force general and Harvard Business School professor named Georges Doriot, took a liking to Olsen and coached the neophyte on the best way to approach the ARD board. Doriot counseled him to promise a high, fast return on investment. And he warned Olsen not to tell the board that he was going to build computers.

THE PLAN WITHIN THE PLAN

"*Fortune* magazine said no one had made any money in computers and no one was about to," Olsen recalled. "So we took them out." Instead, the business plan emphasized making transistorized circuit modules and selling them to larger computer companies for testing their machines. It was almost as an afterthought that the proposal mentioned their eventual plan (assuming everything else worked out) to make computers of their own.

To Olsen's vast relief, the ARD board approved his request and, in return for part ownership, advanced the fledgling Digital Equipment Corporation $70,000 in seed money. In late 1957, the young entrepreneurs leased space on the second floor of an old brick woolen mill in Maynard, Massachusetts, and began turning it into an electronics plant. The mill had nearly nine thousand square feet of space crisscrossed with rafters, pipes and confusing stairways. The partners — now including Olsen's brother Stan, who would handle marketing — pitched in with the sort of zeal that would become characteristic of the new company. "We did most of the work ourselves," Ken Olsen recalled — "painting, cleaning the johns, moving machines."

From the beginning, DEC was patterned after M.I.T. — the organization its founders knew best. Not only did Olsen hire M.I.T. engineers, but he gave them hours and vacations identical to the university's. Olsen believed that people would work hard if given their freedom. DEC's atmosphere was informal, and Olsen encouraged both individual responsibility and teamwork. He let each staff member choose what to work on: Groups of engineers formed around projects, making their own decisions about schedules and technical details.

The mill quickly came alive in its new incarnation. DEC's first line of test modules sold well, and after only 12 months the company turned a modest profit. When Olsen showed the results to Doriot, he was surprised at the response. The general looked at the financial statement and scowled. "I'm sorry to see this," Doriot said. "No one has ever succeeded this soon and survived."

But survive DEC did. After three years of building test modules, the company came out with its first full-blown computer, the PDP-1, in 1960. Its name, Programmed Data Processor, followed policy and omitted the threatening term "computer," but there was no mistaking the new machine's identity. It was a

The whimsically named Has Beens, a softball team of Digital Equipment Corporation employees, includes company founder Ken Olsen *(fourth from left)* in this mid-1960s photograph. Informality was a hallmark of DEC's early years; after a 1964 reorganization, some of the firm's original members quit rather than put up with the new, stricter hierarchy.

computer, even if most users had never seen anything quite like it. At the time, most computers were million-dollar, one-ton behemoths that required an air-conditioned room and a staff of experts to run properly. The $120,000 PDP-1, by contrast, weighed 250 pounds, took up four six-foot-high cabinets, needed no special cooling and could be handled by a single user with only a little training. It offered more speed per dollar than any other computer of the time.

The PDP-1 was a solid, if not spectacular, success. For several years, DEC designed and introduced new computers at the rate of nearly one a year, always with more power at less cost. Computers in the PDP line quickly became DEC's main product: fast machines that were both smaller and cheaper than anything else around. They filled an overlooked market niche by giving small organizations computing power they could afford.

Initially, the company concentrated on production and avoided developing large sales and service forces. DEC was counting on a knowledgeable customer base—users such as engineers and research scientists, who were familiar with computers and did not demand the kind of software and maintenance services offered by a big company like IBM. But more and more commercial businesses bought machines in the PDP line, and DEC's service component had to grow. The company recognized the need to make operating procedures less intimidating to users who were not technically trained. Engineering vice president Gordon Bell devised what he called the "Mary Jane test": Prototype machines were given to his secretary to try out. If she found a switch inconveniently placed or had any trouble running the computer, back it went for revision.

As DEC began its push toward prominence in the computer industry, it held fast to the basic principles reflected in Olsen's founding philosophy: "Growth is not our primary goal. After making a good product, growth is a natural occurrence." Olsen's financial strategy was conservative. When DEC was born, his immediate aim was to produce a return on ARD's investment, while avoiding further debt and plowing all profits into the development of new and better machines. He also chose not to accept military contracts, a stance that some observers found utterly bewildering. Such contracts could contribute mightily to the financial security of the new company, but Olsen believed military funds were "too easy to come by" and would inhibit DEC's efforts in the civilian arena.

A SMALL WONDER

In 1965, the company hit a bonanza: Its desk-top PDP-8, with a price of about $18,000, proved an instant success. For the first time, users could get a fast computer that was cheap enough to be devoted to one job if necessary, small enough to fit in an already crowded lab or office, and simple enough to be used by nonexperts. In the era of miniskirts, it was perhaps inevitable that the small machine was quickly dubbed a minicomputer. The PDP-8 would become an archetype in the industry and boost its maker into the front ranks of computer manufacturers; by the 1980s, DEC had sold 50,000 of the machines.

The PDP-8 cost about one fifth as much as the IBM 360, a much larger and faster computer introduced about the same time. For users who found that their jobs did not require the power of the IBM machine, the DEC offering held great appeal. As word of the PDP-8 spread, DEC's puny marketing staff could not keep pace with the demand. Some would-be buyers called the company directly to place orders rather than trying to deal with the overburdened sales force. Recalled one competitor: "DEC had a super machine but you had to find them, go up to Maynard and beat on the mill door."

Soon enough, a host of competitors rushed to seize a share of the small-computer market. In addition to established electronics firms, these challengers included start-up ventures looking to emulate DEC's quick success. One such newcomer, Data General, knew the details of that success very well: It was founded by former DEC engineers. But in the minicomputer field, DEC was so far out in front that the only competition was for second place. In 1969, DEC consolidated its domination with the unveiling of its PDP-11 family; the basic model delivered twice the speed of the original PDP-8 for about the same price. By the early 1970s, Olsen's firm controlled 34 percent of the minicomputer market—more than its three biggest competitors (Honeywell, Hewlett-Packard and IBM) combined.

Minis dramatically broadened the use of computers, taking on jobs that often had little to do with traditional number crunching and data processing. The Chicago Police Department, for example, used a PDP-11 to keep track of the 4.5 million telephone calls received each year on its 911 emergency line. Laboratories used minicomputers to control instruments and record experimental results; in the publishing industry they were the brains of electronic typesetting systems; and in automobile plants they directed welding machines and kept track of parts inventories. Minis organized mailing lists and ran machinery that picked potatoes and sorted trash. As computing grew increasingly decentralized, factories, banks, department stores and offices could use the versatile machines to automate in small doses. The age of the minis was in full flower, and so was DEC.

A NEW LINE OF ATTACK

Despite the utility of minicomputers, they did have their limitations. Computationally intensive problems in such fields as seismology and astrophysics might take months to run on a mini. This unacceptably long wait could be avoided by using a supercomputer such as the CDC 6600, but computing time on these scarce machines was too expensive for most research budgets. In the 1970s, a new market began to take shape around the demand for low-cost machines specifically designed to crunch numbers in scientific applications. Limited at first, the market was nevertheless inviting to hungry entrepreneurs. One of the earliest ventures was Floating Point Systems (FPS), an Oregon firm whose success story was a small-scale version of DEC's.

FPS owed its name to the company's first product, a peripheral device (designed to be connected to a mainframe or minicomputer) called a floating-point processor. The processor had specialized hardware that allowed it to do floating-point calculations *(page 40)* much faster than the general-purpose host computer. Scientists referred to the processors as "stunt boxes" for the spectacular speed improvements — on the order of 10 times — that they brought to large mathematical operations.

It was an idea for a new kind of stunt box that had launched FPS. In early 1970, a group of engineers at Tektronix, an electronic instruments maker in Portland, Oregon, decided to try starting a company to build floating-point processors that could be attached to any computer. Seeking management help and funding for the business, they approached Norman Winningstad, a former colleague who had recently left the company to go to business school. Winningstad agreed to join the enterprise as manager and mechanical designer, bringing with him a nest egg derived from stock he had received as a key employee at Tektronix. In January of 1971, Floating Point Systems sublet part of a World War II Quonset hut in Beaverton, Oregon, moving in with a staff of four. Soon FPS moved right back out; Winningstad's engineers complained that the primitive facilities — part of the floor was dirt — were making it hard to attract staff. The company's new quarters, in a nearby commercial park, were more comfortable if not more dignified: The space below FPS's loft was occupied by a poodle-grooming parlor.

By June 1971, FPS was shipping its first line of floating-point processors. They sold for between $5,000 and $10,000 each, significantly below the price of similar devices offered by competing firms. Sales were steady but not spectacular. Winningstad later recalled that when FPS attended its first trade fair later that year, the firm was still too poor to afford partitions for its booth. Instead, it made do with paper curtains and a rack of its floating-point processors. The specifications and prices listed on the hand-lettered sign attracted customers, however, and they were sufficiently impressed by the numbers to overlook the amateurish way the product was presented.

The company turned a profit in its second year, but its struggles were far from over. Like many new ventures, the firm remained seriously undercapitalized. Winningstad, his savings depleted, took out a mortgage on his house to raise

Workers on Digital Equipment Corporation's production line test circuit boards for the company's PDP-8 computers in the mid-1960s. The testing stations were connected to a completed PDP-8, which checked the circuit boards at each stage of assembly by using its own diagnostic programs.

additional funds. Things looked so bleak, he remembered, that "my wife asked me at the time if I thought the company was going to make it." He was able to assuage her fears but could not deny that there was plenty of reason for uncertainty. At about this time, many computer makers were beginning to build floating-point hardware directly into their machines, undercutting the need for peripheral processors of the type sold by FPS. What Winningstad called "a nice little 10 to 20 million dollar company" was in danger of being swamped.

As it happened, the company was spared. In 1973, the Arab oil embargo rudely shocked the United States into recognizing the vulnerability of its petroleum supply, and FPS suddenly found its products in high demand. For some time, computers had been employed in the search for new reserves *(pages 26-27)*. Now, with American motorists fuming in long lines at service stations, the oil industry made finding new sources of domestic petroleum its top priority.

The search would require a quick infusion of computing power. None of the oil producers owned supercomputers — the introduction of the Cray-1 was still two years away — but many had been using FPS floating-point processors in the manipulation of seismic data. In discussions with FPS, the oil companies made it clear that they would welcome other kinds of peripheral processors to further soup up the performance of a minicomputer or a mainframe; they wanted their machines to be able to process large arrays of seismic data at very high speeds.

FPS was already developing a product that could do this work. Called an array processor, or AP, it would use special hardware and software to tackle the mathematically intensive parts of a program handed to it by the host computer. Far more complex than a floating-point processor, the planned array processor would have its own memory and be programmable to take on a variety of jobs. But when the oil crisis struck, the prototype of the new machine was at least nine months from completion. With no time to waste, George O'Leary, the designer of the FPS array processor, recommended that the project be put aside. Instead, the company licensed a design for an array processor developed several years earlier by a former math professor in California named Glen Culler. Culler's device, originally intended to do the specialized mathematical functions needed in speech synthesis, was ideal for rapidly carrying out quantities of repetitive calculations. The secret of this speed lay in the AP's architecture, which allowed different operations to be performed on many pieces of data simultaneously. FPS improved Culler's design by breaking down the arithmetic operations into an assembly-line organization called a pipeline (pages 58-59), and by changing some internal features to simplify programming.

With the design modification under way, FPS rapidly shifted gears. In 1974, the company stopped putting money into floating-point hardware, spending it instead on developing its new product line. The first array processor, the AP-120B, came to market in 1975. When hooked to a mini for special operations such as analysis of seismic data, it made the system as fast as any machine except a supercomputer. No bigger than a small filing cabinet, the AP-120B could easily be moved from place to place; petroleum prospectors armed with a mini and an AP would be able to perform sophisticated analysis in the field. The oil companies were elated, and so was FPS as the orders poured in.

A NEW STANDARD
Like DEC's PDP-8, Floating Point System's AP-120B became a benchmark in the industry and secured the company's reputation as a leader. Speed was not the machine's only virtue; the AP could be programmed to match different needs, tackling a variety of math-intensive scientific problems. For example, modeling dynamic events — the air flow around a jet, a storm pattern over a coast, or stress on a building — requires highly repetitive calculations for many data points, corresponding to the shape of the structure or system being modeled. These and kindred applications proved ideally suited to the AP-120B, whose modest cost (as low as $30,000 for the basic unit) put it within reach of university scientists.

One scientist who recognized the revolutionary potential of the array processor was Kenneth Wilson, a Cornell University physicist. Wilson had recently developed a new computational approach to understanding physical systems involving numerous bodies separated by distances that varied greatly in magnitude. His method, which could be applied to many fields of study — and for which he would eventually win a Nobel Prize — usually required substantial computing power. In 1978, Wilson drew several other Cornell scientists into a computing consortium. The researchers pooled their funds to buy an AP-190L, FPS's newest model of array processor. Two astrophysicists, Stuart Shapiro and Saul Teukolsky, gave the machine one of its first jobs: investigating the mysterious objects known as black holes.

The events leading to the formation of a black hole comprise one of the most complex and exotic puzzles that a computer had ever been called on to answer. Once a star has exhausted its nuclear fuel, it begins to fall inward under the force of gravity. If a star is big enough (at least three times as massive as the sun, which is about 864,000 miles in diameter), the force of its collapse may compress all of its matter into a sphere less than four miles across. Scientists call this object a black hole because nothing — not even light — can escape the immense gravitational field created by so much matter so densely packed.

Black holes, by definition, cannot be directly observed; thus, scientists' understanding of them is purely theoretical. Using equations derived from Einstein's general theory of relativity and focusing on simplified scenarios, they can work out a qualitative description of the processes surrounding a star's catastrophic transformation into a black hole. But anything more detailed requires a powerful computer. To try to understand the dynamics of a massive star in the last stages of life, astrophysicists create a mathematical model of it, with the goal of determining the movement of the stellar fluid through space and time. Such a model may consist of dozens of interconnected equations and millions of data values representing the positions of particles and their speed and direction.

The problems of working with fluid systems like the interior of a star have to do with what scientists call nonlinearities. Basically, the particles or other elements in a nonlinear system cannot be treated as independent entities that behave in a neatly predictable manner. Rather, each part of the system is continually influenced by the motion of other parts. The cumulative effect of all this interaction does not grow at a constant rate; it may amplify very rapidly, outstripping the calculating ability of all but the fastest computers.

Before the arrival of the array processor, the Cornell astrophysicists had been unable to do this "numerical experimentation." The university's biggest computer — an IBM 370/168 — was too busy and too expensive to use on such time-consuming, math-intensive problems. But attaching the AP-190L to the IBM computer created a hybrid that tackled the black-hole problem with ease. Shapiro and Teukolsky gained fresh perspectives on the behavior of matter and gravity and even produced a film that used computer output to graphically portray a collapsing star. Similar exercises, dealing with the evolution of galaxies and the physics of extremely dense matter, were equally accessible. In addition to being six times as fast as the host computer working by itself, the AP brought the cost of heavy numerical computation into the affordable range: $10 to $40 per hour, as opposed to $500 to $1,500 per hour for the same job performed on the much more expensive IBM 370/168.

MORE SPEED PER DOLLAR
Other universities began buying array processors and were soon trumpeting their effectiveness. Physicists from the University of California at Los Angeles compared the cost of their processor with time-sharing charges on the university's mainframe and found the array processor 200 times cheaper. Another study compared the efficiency of an array processor to that of a supercomputer: When the cost of the AP was divided by its raw speed — the number of floating-point operations per second — the processor had seven times more speed per dollar and was only two and a half times slower. In Wilson's opinion, the AP provided "spectacularly cost-effective computing — almost always better than any other computer, from microcomputers to a Cray-1."

To the rest of the computer industry, Floating Point Systems seemed to have come out of nowhere. Riding the crest of the AP wave, Winningstad watched the size of his company quadruple in 1976 and again in 1977 before merely doubling in 1978, when it went public and brought instant wealth to its cofounders.

By 1981, net annual sales were approaching $60 million. A host of other companies were following the FPS lead in the production of array processors, which were employed in fields as diverse as flight simulation, meteorology, pollution control, medical CAT scans and the operation of nuclear plants.

During this period, the distinctions between different types of computers gradually eroded. Some companies began marketing "superminis," small machines that far exceeded the power of the old PDP series. Even more powerful machines, often incorporating such architectural features as vector processing, also entered the market and were dubbed "minisupers" or "baby Crays."

In 1981, FPS further blurred the lines when it began marketing machines that it called scientific computers. Like array processors, these new machines were designed to be linked to a general-purpose computer, but there the resemblance ended. Where array processors worked only on the heavily numerical parts of programs, scientific computers were intended to handle entire programs at a speed approaching that of a supercomputer. The host computer served mainly to handle the prosaic tasks of program development and input and output — "byte-shuffling" in the words of FPS's Winningstad. At a cost of about $400,000, these computers offered the best ratio of price to performance in the industry.

In 1985, after only 10 years in the race to build fast computers, Floating Point Systems reached a new pinnacle of success. In October of that year, Cornell University opened its Center for Theory and Simulation, one of five federally supported supercomputing centers. The brainchild of Kenneth Wilson, the center was the first of its kind not to rely on traditional supercomputers such as the Cray-2. The processing power was provided instead by five FPS scientific computers linked to an IBM 3081 mainframe. Working in parallel, the machines could solve many problems with the speed of a supercomputer, at a fraction of the cost. While the opening of the center was a coup for FPS, winning it recognition as a contender in the supercomputing race, the ceremony's significance was broader still. It marked the coming of age of a whole class of computers that are bringing economical, high-speed computing to thousands of laboratories and companies around the world.

Manipulating
Massive
Models

Among the math-intensive tasks that are a supercomputer's forte, one of the most challenging is that of simulating the behavior of large, complex systems impossible to study with real-world experiments — for instance, the drift of continents over millions of years or, as illustrated on the following pages, global climate and weather patterns. The natural forces that govern these phenomena are immense, numerous and intricately interwoven. Even at supercomputer speeds, climate analysis programs can take more than 100 hours of computer time to run.

To carry out such studies, researchers build mathematical models. Like a mechanical model of a steam engine, a mathematical model duplicates the actions of its real-world counterpart — not with wheels and pistons but with equations. In the case of climate or weather models, the equations are drawn from fundamental laws of physics that show the relationships among variations in wind, sun, temperature, humidity and many other factors. These physical laws serve as the underlying framework into which scientists fit actual data about the atmosphere — millions of measurements taken at a given time and in a given place. This start-up data, as it is called, provides the model with the initial conditions from which its equations will calculate conditions at a later time.

A number of different models have been developed for weather and climate studies, some simulating the earth's climate globally, others replicating localized weather that may affect no more than a square mile. Already such models have improved everyday weather forecasting. By examining the workings of storms that give birth to tornadoes, for instance, they contribute to more timely warnings of these vicious storms. Researchers are using climate models to look into the past, to recreate ancient climates, perhaps eventually to solve such mysteries as the demise of dinosaurs. Most important, the climate models are a key tool for assessing the future, to see how man-made pollution might trigger climatic change, with results that could range from a plague of skin cancer to bountiful fertility in Siberia.

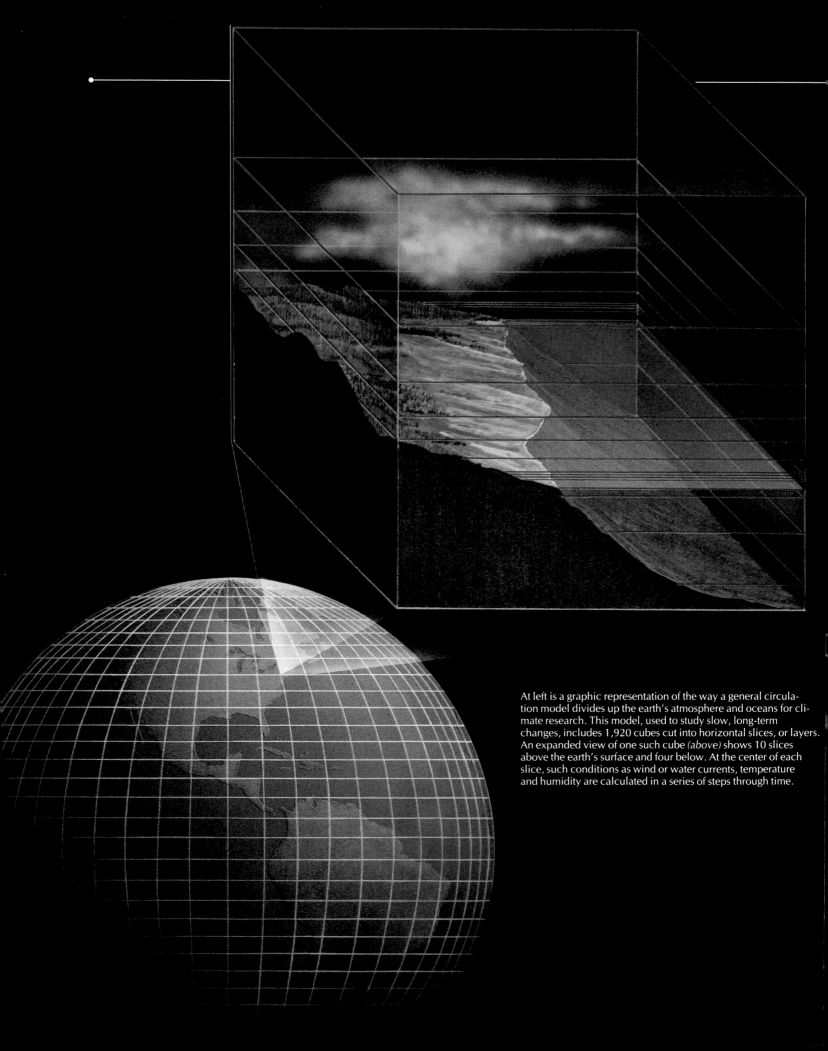

At left is a graphic representation of the way a general circulation model divides up the earth's atmosphere and oceans for climate research. This model, used to study slow, long-term
changes, includes 1,920 cubes cut into horizontal slices, or layers.
An expanded view of one such cube *(above)* shows 10 slices
above the earth's surface and four below. At the center of each
slice, such conditions as wind or water currents, temperature
and humidity are calculated in a series of steps through time.

Taking a Global View

The most complex and realistic of meteorological models give scientists a picture of the atmosphere and oceans worldwide. Called general circulation models (GCMs), they serve for weather forecasting, climate studies and computerized experiments. They can answer such questions as "What happens if the carbon dioxide content of the atmosphere is doubled?" (The global mean temperature of the earth rises a few degrees.) Or "How is climate affected by large amounts of dust and smoke?" (The earth gets much colder.)

In a general circulation model, the atmosphere is divided into a three-dimensional grid, resembling boxes stacked atop and alongside one another. The ocean, which is an important determinant of climate, can be represented in a variety of ways. Relatively crude models ignore the important effects of ocean heat storage and transport; more-developed models include these and other ocean processes. Supplied with start-up data such as temperature, barometric pressure and wind speed and direction, the computer uses the model's equations to calculate changes in weather conditions at the center of horizontal planes within each box.

The model's resolution, or accuracy, depends on the designated length of time between calculations and on the number of points at which calculations are made. The higher the resolution, the greater the cost: Doubling the number of points and halving the simulated time between calculations increases the running time of a GCM sixteenfold. Regional weather forecasting may require 40,000 grid boxes and hour-by-hour computations, while generalized climate studies can manage with 2,000 boxes and day-to-day calculations. This saving in computer time for climate research is often achieved by "parameterization": Instead of using actual data to describe local conditions such as thunderclouds, the model employs a general statistical relationship between these conditions and the atmosphere as a whole.

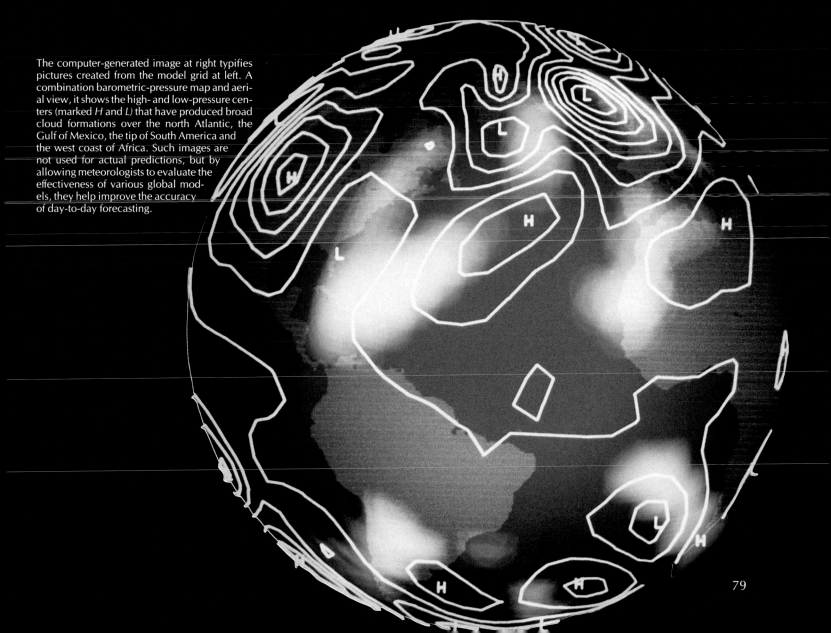

The computer-generated image at right typifies pictures created from the model grid at left. A combination barometric-pressure map and aerial view, it shows the high- and low-pressure centers (marked *H* and *L*) that have produced broad cloud formations over the north Atlantic, the Gulf of Mexico, the tip of South America and the west coast of Africa. Such images are not used for actual predictions, but by allowing meteorologists to evaluate the effectiveness of various global models, they help improve the accuracy of day-to-day forecasting.

Replicas of the Past and Future

With the masses of data that general circulation models manipulate, scientists can perform computer experiments in simulating both ancient climates and future ones. Because the natural mechanisms that affect climate are imperfectly understood, a given simulation can only suggest the approximate magnitude and location of changes brought about by altering various elements of the model. Despite these handicaps, climate models stand up reasonably well when compared against real-world observations.

One study, by the National Center for Atmospheric Research (NCAR) in Boulder, Colorado, has examined the long-term impact of atmospheric pollution resulting mainly from carbon dioxide gas (CO_2) given off by burning fuels. The atmosphere naturally contains carbon dioxide — from sources such as volcanoes, decaying plants and other chemical processes — which helps trap heat from the sun through the greenhouse effect *(below)*. But over the past century, human use of fuels has greatly added to atmospheric CO_2, and if the increase continues at its current rate, the present concentration is expected to double between the years 2050 and 2100.

Using a global circulation model, researchers at NCAR plugged in data to represent a doubling of the carbon dioxide level and then ran the program to project climatic conditions over a span of 11 years. Even at the rate of 80 million calculations per second, computing the results required 132 hours on a Cray-1: twelve hours for every model year. The charts at right, based on two-dimensional computer graphics generated by the program, show an average of the results from the last three years of simulation during the months of December, January and February.

In the greenhouse effect, solar energy *(yellow arrow)* easily penetrates the earth's atmosphere. But reflected heat, in the form of infrared radiation, is absorbed by gases and water vapor *(short orange arrow),* and only a little escapes *(long arrow).* With more CO_2 in the atmosphere. more heat is trapped.

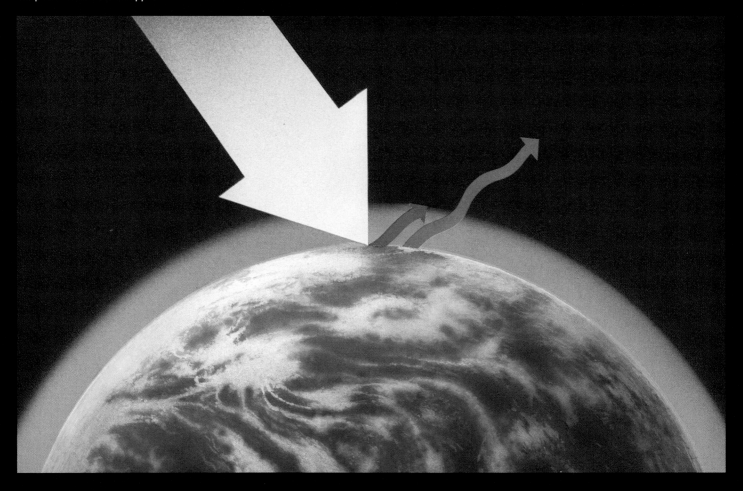

The Consequences of Doubled CO_2

A general warming
Numbered lines indicate average winter temperature changes eight to 11 years after doubling today's levels of atmospheric CO_2. The model shows increases as high as 16° C. (29° F.) near the poles, where sea ice would recede in the warmer climate, while the equatorial rise is only 2° C. (3.6° F.).

Melting ice caps
This illustration depicts the way polar ice would recede *(dashed lines)* from present levels *(solid lines)*. Melting ice would not only expand oceans and inundate cities along the coastlines, it would increase the amount of water that is exposed to the sun's heat and raise ocean temperatures.

DJF CONTROL
DJF 2 x CO_2

Changing soil moisture levels
Doubling CO_2 tends to increase precipitation in winter, especially in the middle latitudes. As indicated by lines tracing changes (in centimeters of precipitation), soil moisture levels, which are crucial to agriculture, would rise in much of Europe, Asia and Canada. But in Africa, Indonesia and the southern U.S., moisture levels may drop.

A Cooling Theory

When dinosaurs roamed the earth 65 million years ago during the Cretaceous period, global temperatures were about 14° C. (25° F.) higher than now. One theory attributes the subsequent cooling off solely to continental drift: Land masses then *(red)* were closer to the equator than they are today *(gray)*, and warm ocean currents would have kept ice off the poles. But testing the idea in a GCM showed temperature changes of less than 5° C. (9° F.). Testing higher CO_2 levels — caused by volcanic activity, for example — might give more significant results.

Pinpointing the Source of Acid Rain

Checking the model's predictions

To test their acid-rain model, researchers ran simulations of a rainstorm, using data from an actual storm that occurred in late April of 1981. The three maps directly below show, left to right, simulated rainfall *(blue)* 24, 48 and 72 hours after the storm began — a good match with real rain measured at those times and places.

Acid rain (a shorthand term for acid deposition in all its forms, including snow and fog) is blamed for harming forests, lakes and rivers across the northeastern United States, Canada and Scandinavia. Its apparent sources are industrial smokestacks and automobile exhausts, which emit fumes containing sulfur, nitrogen and hydrocarbons. These chemicals then react with oxidants in the air to form acids that are carried away by winds and deposited across the globe. The chief culprits, many experts believe, are power plants and smelters that burn coal containing sulfur. (In North America, a principal concentration of such industry occurs in the Ohio Valley, while Scandinavia is vulnerable

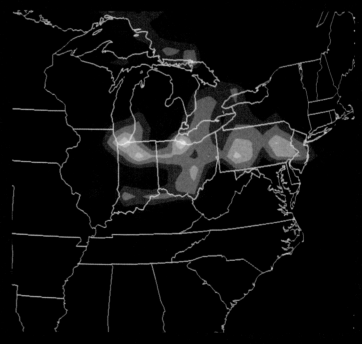

Following the fallout

The three maps above track the accumulation of acid rain *(yellow marks heaviest depositions)* as simulated for times corresponding to those of the rainfall mapped in the top row. Start-up data for the

simulation was based on actual measurements of sulfur emissions, and the simulation was checked against ground observations of the acid fallout. The results proved reasonably accurate, particularly early in the test, before inevitable errors accumulated.

to the smokestacks of Great Britain and Eastern Europe.)

Scientists studying the problem at the National Center for Atmospheric Research are working to devise an accurate computer model of the way pollutants interact with the atmosphere and move about. Their chemical transport model, one of the most complex in the atmospheric sciences, covers the northeastern United States with grid boxes 80 kilometers square (nearly 2,500 square miles) and extending to an average altitude of 14 kilometers (just under nine miles). It integrates two components: One is a meteorological model similar to the example illustrated on page 78; the other is a chemical model that incorporates equations representing chemical reactions along with documented emissions of pollutants such as hydrocarbons, sulfur dioxide and nitrogen oxide. Run on a Cray X-MP, the model simulates the hour-by-hour transformation of pollutants as they rise, mix into the atmosphere and eventually return to the ground. (The results shown below are at 24-hour intervals.)

Acid deposition is only one of several problems to which the chemical transport model can be applied. As investigators refine its various elements over time, the basic model can be adapted to a range of regional and global pollution problems, including studies of urban smog and the impact that increases in CO_2 may have upon the environment.

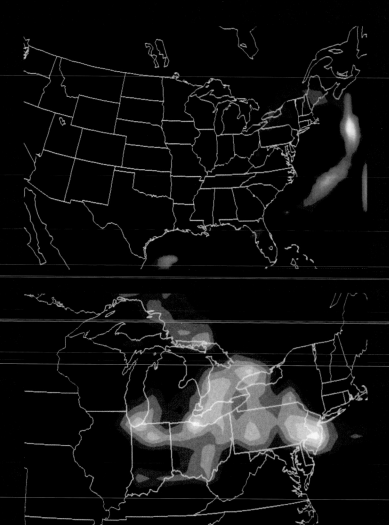

Reduced Sulfur, Less Acid

Once the tests documented at left established that the model could reliably predict acid deposition, researchers tested the fundamental question: Would reducing sulfur emissions in the Ohio Valley significantly reduce acid rain far away? The answer is in the map above. It shows the simulation of fallout from the same April rainstorm after 72 hours, but in this case the start-up data has been changed in one respect: The amount of sulfur pollutants entering the atmosphere has been cut in half. Here the diffusion of red, marking acid deposition, covers less territory than it does in the map of the test with full-strength pollution *(left)*, and the virtual absence of yellow indicates that deposits were lighter as well.

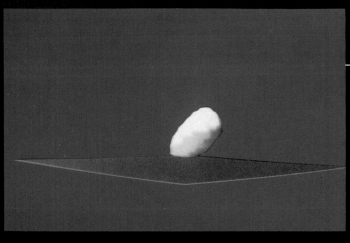

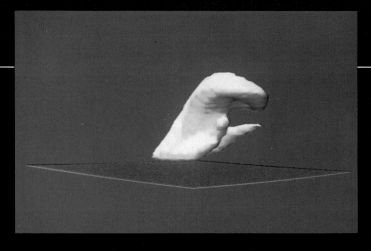

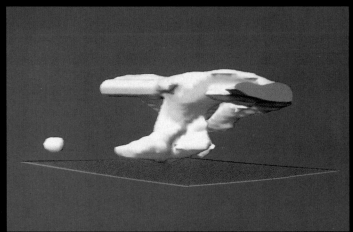

From puff cloud to tornado-maker
A thunderstorm's evolution is traced clockwise from upper left in these computer images. Starting as a small cloud close to earth *(green)*, the storm at 30 minutes is taller and has begun to develop a typical "anvil" top. At 60 minutes, a "flanking line" starts to stretch left, while precipitation *(blue shading)* forms, and downdrafts begin to spread out beneath the storm. At 100 minutes, the anvil is more pronounced. At two hours *(below)*, a "wall cloud" has lowered — a frequent tornado signal.

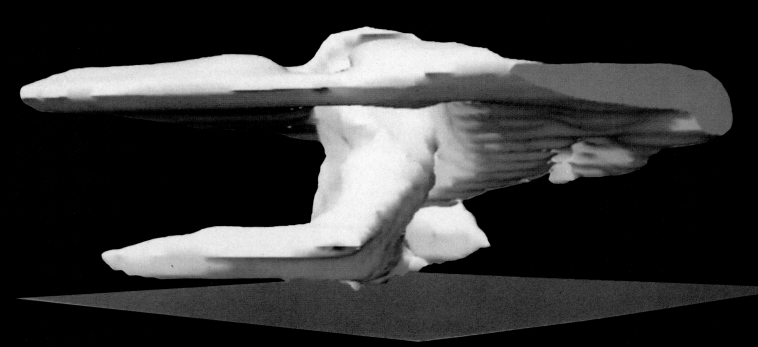

The Birth of a Thunderstorm

In an average day, the atmosphere spawns 45,000 thunderstorms—huge dark clouds that may be 50 miles wide and 10 miles high. Such storms are dangerous, giving rise to deadly tornadoes *(following pages),* lashing the earth with lightning that kills 200 people a year in the United States and dropping hail that costs U.S. farmers a billion dollars annually in crop damage.

Understanding how thunderstorms work is obviously important if timely warnings are to be issued. It is also extremely difficult. Radar has helped to explain the behavior of the storms, its beams looking inside the towering clouds to reveal their inner structure. But essential thermodynamic details such as temperature and pressure are almost impossible to record: Thunderstorms go by quickly, and instruments are sometimes pounded into uselessness by winds and debris.

With the advent of very powerful computers and sophisticated, interactive graphics software, scientists can now use computer modeling to get around these difficulties. Although the models are enormously complex, generating masses of data for any segment of a simulated storm, researchers can convert the data into realistic images on a video screen. By keying in commands to display specific kinds of information, such as color-coded maps of wind directions at various levels within a cloud *(below),* scientists can examine details of a storm's make-up that they might otherwise miss—and all in a matter of seconds.

Examining a cloud's interior
Slicing through a thunderstorm, computer images display its features at ground level, four kilometers (2.4 miles) and eight kilometers (4.8 miles). White arrows mark horizontal winds, red and green contours show updrafts and downdrafts, blue shading represents precipitation, and the yellow line the boundary between cold and warm air at ground level. In the middle level, precipitation around the indented updrafts—a "hook echo"—presages a tornado.

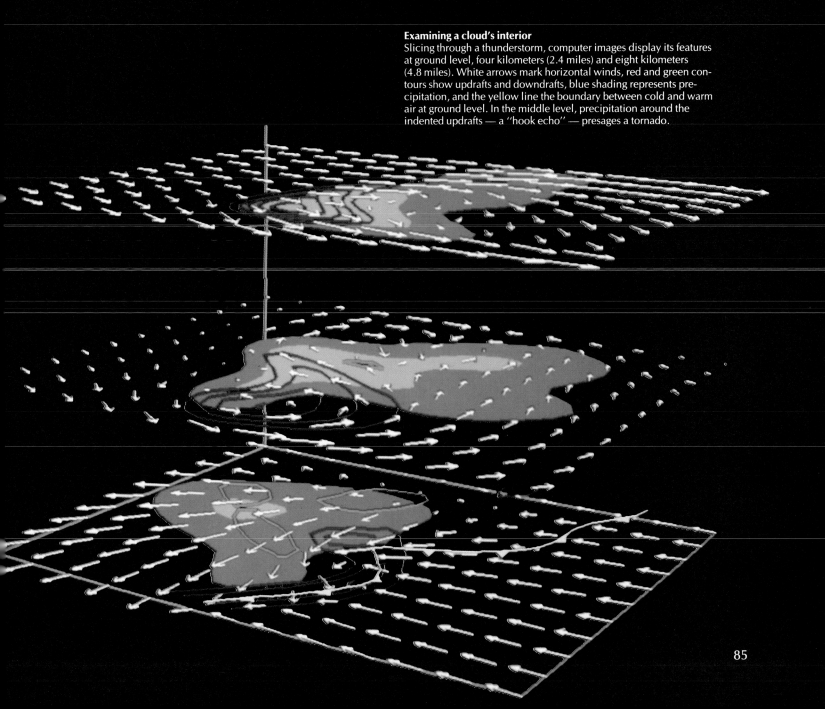

Tracing a Tornado's Evolution

The ominous black funnel of a tornado dips suddenly from a thundercloud, roars across a few feet or a few miles and as suddenly disappears, gone generally in less than 15 minutes. More than 640 of these deadly twisters strike the United States in an average year — about half of them in Tornado Alley, a 400-mile swath of land stretching from Texas north to Missouri. They cause property damage averaging $50 million annually and over the course of a half century have killed some 9,000 people.

With better understanding of thunderstorms, largely obtained from computer models, forecasters hope to improve the accuracy and lead time of tornado watches and tornado warnings. One such model helped NCAR researchers create diagrams *(right)* that explain how a tornado develops. The model simulated the evolution of a storm *(below)* within a volume of atmosphere 55 kilometers square by 16 kilometers high (34 by 34 by 10 miles). This volume is divided into a grid of nearly 100,000 boxes, each representing parcels of air one kilometer square by half a kilometer high. Then, combining the physical equations that govern atmospheric motion, temperature, pressure, moisture and other characteristics, the computer calculates changes within each parcel every six seconds.

As complex as it is, even this model cannot simulate a tornado within a storm: Typically only several hundred meters wide, a tornado is smaller than a single grid box. What the model can do is produce a series of images that reveal how one type of severe storm, the supercell thunderstorm, can generate the strong rotation that leads to tornadoes. The supercell thunderstorm contains violent rotating updrafts that may reach 100 miles per hour. This intense, tornadic rotation develops rapidly, usually near the end of the storm's life.

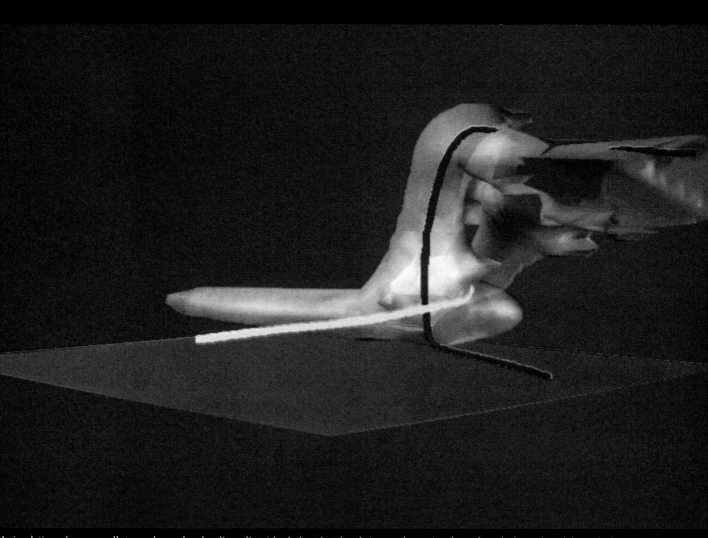

A simulation of a supercell storm shows the cloud's outline *(shaded)* and paths of air parcels passing through updrafts *(red)* and downdrafts *(yellow)*.

Where the Spin Begins

This drawing, based on a computer model of a supercell storm, shows early stages of rotation. Wind shear (arrows, far left) — easterly winds becoming westerly higher up — produces horizontal rotation (four small orange arrows). This spinning air forms vortex tubes that are tilted vertical as they are swept into the updraft (yellow), making two vortices that spiral in opposite directions (plus and minus signs). Precipitation (blue lines) weakens the updraft, but rotation promotes new updrafts at the side (purple arrows).

After the supercell thunderstorm matures, low-level rotation intensifies. At this point in the simulation, a gust front (barbed blue line) — a boundary of cold air beneath the storm — causes vortex tubes to turn directly toward the storm center and converge into it. As these vortex tubes are tilted up into the storm, powerful rotation develops rapidly beneath the cloud — precursor to a tornado.

88

The Promise of Parallelism

In the late 1970s, Cray Research, with its Cray-1, was the unquestioned champion of supercomputing; Control Data Corporation and its Cyber 203 offered Cray's only significant competition. The two firms' domination of the high-speed computer market carried on the long-standing tradition of American leadership in the field. But on the other side of the Pacific, the Japanese were quietly readying an assault on that leadership. By early 1979, a committee of university researchers, backed by $400,000 from the Japanese Ministry of International Trade and Industry (MITI), had begun a program of intensive study of high-speed computing. Over the next two years, the group's members pored over technical literature from a multitude of international sources. They invited Western experts — primarily leading researchers in artificial intelligence (AI) from M.I.T., Carnegie Mellon and Stanford — to speak about developments at the cutting edge of computer science. The committee also produced nearly 2,000 pages of reports describing the most promising avenues of investigation.

Then, in October 1981, at a conference in Tokyo, the Japanese revealed the results of their research blitz: a dramatic plan to leapfrog current technology and secure the world lead in advanced computing by the late 1990s. One part of the plan, the National Superspeed computer project, would spend an estimated $200 million over eight years to develop a supercomputer capable of executing 10 gigaflops, or 10 billion floating-point operations per second — 65 times faster than the Cray-1. The second prong of the attack was the even more ambitious Fifth Generation project. (Vacuum tubes, transistors, integrated circuits, and very-large-scale integrated circuits represent the technologies of the first through the fourth generation, respectively.) Expected to run 10 years and cost $500 million, the program was designed to achieve breakthroughs in AI technology and incorporate them in computers that would, among other skills, be able to understand natural human language. It was a breathtaking proposal. Alluding to the successful maiden flight of the space shuttle earlier in the year, Tohru Motooka, the electrical engineering professor who headed the committee that wrote the plan, declared that the project "aims to be the space shuttle of the knowledge world. We want to prove the economic viability of challenging the unknown."

As the implications of the Japanese challenge sank in, other countries began organizing a response. Supercomputers represent a relatively small market, but they have a dual strategic value. The technological advances brought to fruition in these elite machines tend to filter down into the rest of the industry; thus, whoever leads in supercomputing tends to lead in other areas of computing as well. Perhaps more important from the standpoint of national security, high-speed computers are crucial to the design of new weapons systems and the making and breaking of codes used in military and intelligence activities.

Collectively and separately, the nations of Western Europe and the Communist bloc drew up plans that earmarked billions of dollars for their own supercomputing projects. But perhaps nowhere was the reaction to Japan's announcement more intense than in the United States. Granted, some industry executives regarded the Tokyo declarations as "a lot of smoke," particularly the AI goal of producing computers endowed with near-human reason and sensory perception: Western researchers had been pursuing the goal of intelligent machines for well over two decades, and the Japanese were neophytes. But another segment of the microelectronics industry was seriously concerned about the country's potential loss of leadership in the field. In a move totally at odds with the industry's normally cutthroat competition, 12 companies, including Control Data, Honeywell and RCA, banded together in a venture to conduct research and development on a variety of advanced technology projects.

At the same time, several government agencies—the Pentagon, the National Science Foundation (NSF) and the Department of Energy—stepped up research efforts being made on several fronts in conjunction with the academic community. The Defense Advanced Research Projects Agency (DARPA), long a generous supporter of work in artificial intelligence, targeted a number of ambitious AI-related goals, including the development of hardware and software to support autonomous systems and real-time battlefield assessment.

A major NSF project sought to make research scientists and potential computer designers more familiar with supercomputing. In the 1970s, the U.S. had fallen dangerously behind both Europe and Japan in providing university students and researchers access to supercomputers. Not only did this hamper basic research in everything from chemistry and aerodynamics to computer science itself, it produced a generation of students who lacked the training needed to design and operate the most advanced machines. As one industry executive put it, "The best number I've heard is that there are about 250 people in the United States who really understand the monsters."

In 1985, the NSF put up $200 million to establish national supercomputing centers at the University of California at San Diego, Princeton, Cornell and the University of Illinois. These four operations—linked by ground lines and satellites to other universities across the country—started up in July 1985; a fifth center, affiliated with the University of Pittsburgh and Carnegie-Mellon, opened its doors in June 1986. Equipped with supercomputers such as the Cray X-MP and Control Data's Cyber 205, the five national centers were meant not only to encourage university-based researchers to develop new applications, but also to help them rethink the computer and reinvent its architecture.

In short, Japan's vaulting ambitions had started a computer race every bit as far-reaching as the space race precipitated by the launching of the Soviet satellite Sputnik a generation earlier. In laboratories around the world, scientists and engineers began placing their bets on various approaches to building and programming computers that are superfast or supersmart—or both.

MOBILIZING JAPAN, INC.

Japan—or Japan, Inc., as some refer to it—was reckoned a formidable competitor. The nickname was coined by rivals chagrined at the way the country's industry works hand-in-glove with the government. At the heart of Japan, Inc. is MITI, the agency set up in 1949 to guide, protect and, when necessary, bankroll Japanese industry. MITI masterminded Japan's postwar industrial renaissance and, over the years, has been responsible for many of the country's successes in the overseas marketplace—notably in the steel and automobile industries. It was MITI's philosophy of vision-making—a seemingly uncanny ability to peer into the future and isolate an objective of great economic potential—that propelled Japan to the top of the semiconductor market in the 1970s.

Another source of strength for the Japanese computer industry is its typically vertical corporate structure. In the U.S., computer makers generally buy components from independently owned manufacturers; unless the two firms' cycles of design, development and delivery can be made to dovetail, the result may be a lengthy delay in bringing a new computer to market. Unlike their American counterparts, many Japanese computer firms are also leading makers of semiconductors. Consequently, the companies can easily channel research funding into developing whatever custom chips are necessary to achieve their goals, and they orchestrate all phases of the production schedule.

By the mid-1980s, three of the companies participating in the Superspeed and Fifth Generation projects—Hitachi, Fujitsu and Nippon Electric Company (NEC) —had begun marketing supercomputers. Hitachi earlier had pioneered in the development of 256K memory chips, which were for several years the most widely used semiconductor memory. Now Hitachi entered the supercomputing fray with its S810-20, a machine that could barrel along at about 600 megaflops. Fujitsu's VP-400, at 1.14 gigaflops, was nearly twice as fast. But the leader of the pack proved to be NEC's ultrafast SX-2, with an announced peak speed of 1.3 gigaflops. Introduced in 1985, the SX-2 took direct aim at the Cray-2, which also debuted that year.

These speed claims were subject to sometimes acrimonious debate. The absolute switching speed of a computer's electronic components and the arrangement of its wiring are only two of the factors that determine its performance. Among other things, a machine's speed also depends on the kind of problem it is given to run and how well the program takes advantage of the machine's particular architecture *(pages 92-95)*. As Cray president John Rollwagen liked to put it, a supercomputer's peak speed is comparable to the speed of the spinning wheels of a car on blocks: The motion is meaningless unless useful work is being done.

Whatever its ultimate speed, the SX-2 was unquestionably a successful product of Japan's supercomputing efforts. As is typically the case in Japan, the machine was the creation not of one person but of a team, developed through a long process of consensus and compromise. In spite of the prevailing group ethic, however, the SX-2 project was not without a strong hand on the tiller.

Tadashi Watanabe, the head, or *bucho,* of NEC's supercomputer division, was acknowledged the machine's chief architect and—in the words of one NEC executive—"the guy everybody looks to for guidance." Watanabe joined NEC in 1968, immediately after graduating from the University of Tokyo. He spent four years in the firm's software division, followed by stints in various other departments, before being placed in charge of the supercomputer division in the early 1980s, just as NEC was gearing up to produce the SX-2.

Over the next four years, Watanabe guided the SX-2 through the tricky shoals of its development. As he recalled later somewhat ruefully, the machine took shape in the course of "many, many conferences." But as *bucho,* he possessed a certain clout, and if an arbitrary decision was needed to break up a logjam,

The Teamwork Behind Parallel Processing

Even knottier than designing new machines for parallel processing *(pages 64-65)* is coordinating the work they perform. In the examples shown here and on the following pages, teams of painters represent the way parallel processors might collaborate on a variety of tasks. The painters' instructions serve as simplified computer programs, reflecting in each case the most streamlined sequence of commands for the job.

Before the processors can tackle their separate assignments, the overall task must be broken into a set of subtasks

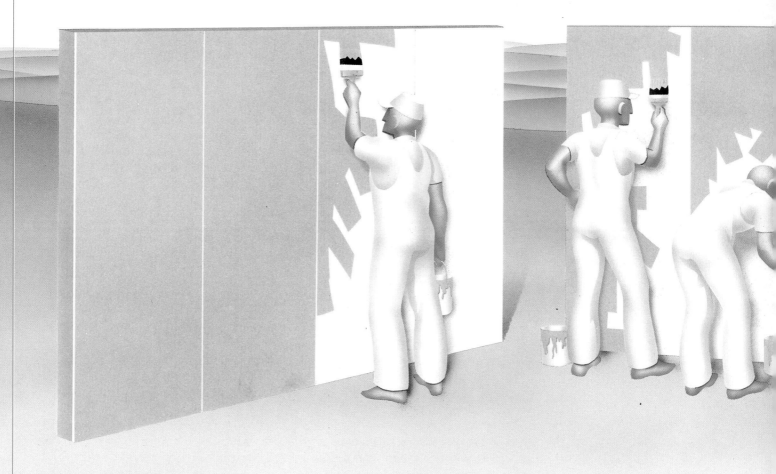

A single painter. Like a single processor running a sequential program, a lone painter can proceed at his own pace in completing the assignment — here, to paint a four-panel wall. Because only one worker is drawing upon the available resources, no instructions are needed to prevent conflict, and the program can be reduced to a single statement *(left)*. The liability of such an approach is its slowness. Its principal advantage is flexibility: The painter need not wait for others before moving to the next task.

PROGRAM 1:

Paint entire wall.

An asynchronous team. Four painters working independently cover the wall in roughly a quarter of the time the single painter needed. But the team can perform only tasks that allow each painter to work without reference to anyone else's progress. Similarly, computing tasks amenable to asynchronous execution are those in which the processors do not require one another's results to carry out their own work. To verify the spelling in a long manuscript, for example, several processors could check one chapter apiece.

and distributed among them. The degree to which paralleliza-tion can accelerate the running of the program depends on how interdependent the subtasks are and how often they re-quire access to the same data. Theoretically, for example, if a lone painter takes one hour to cover a wall, four painters working in parallel should be able to do the job in 15 minutes. But in practice, the need to coordinate activities results in delays — called overhead — that retard linear speed-up.

Overhead comes in several guises. If, for instance, two or more painters must fill their buckets from a common reservoir of paint, they will find themselves vying for the supply at some point. This competition for a single resource is called conten-tion overhead, and in parallel processing it most often takes the form of several processors simultaneously trying to re-trieve the same piece of data from main memory. Other types of overhead include separation and reconstitution — that is, the cost of dividing the work among the various processors, and the cost of merging the results.

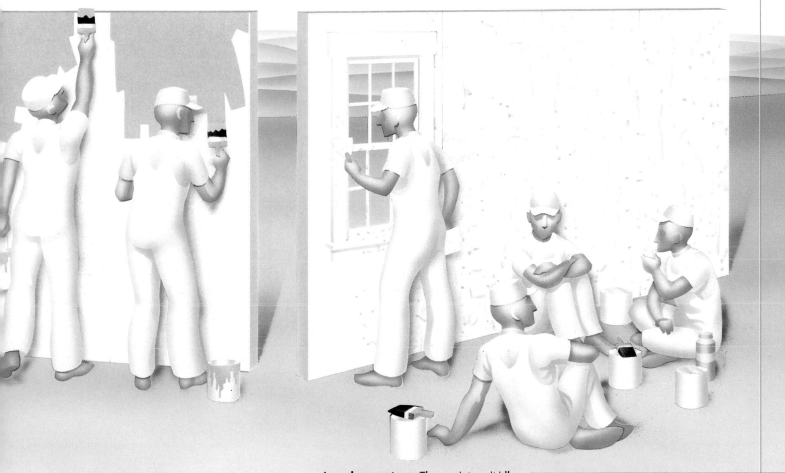

PROGRAM 2:			
PAINTER 1	*PAINTER 2*	*PAINTER 3*	*PAINTER 4*
Paint first part of wall.	Paint second part of wall.	Paint third part of wall.	Paint fourth part of wall.

A synchronous team. Three painters sit idle while their partner finishes the slowest sub-task in a more complex project — scraping and painting a wall interrupted by a window. To avoid getting paint chips in the fresh paint, the workers must all begin the next phase at the same time. For problems such as simulat-ing molecular motion, parallel processors often must await another result in order to cal-culate the forces that propel subatomic par-ticles; the time lost to the synchronization de-pends on the slowest computation.

PROGRAM 3:			
PAINTER 1	*PAINTER 2*	*PAINTER 3*	*PAINTER 4*
Scrape first part of wall.	Scrape second part of wall.	Scrape third part of wall.	Scrape fourth part of wall.
Wait until all scraping is done.	Wait until all scraping is done.	Wait until all scraping is done.	Wait until all scraping is done.
Paint first part of wall.	Paint second part of wall.	Paint third part of wall.	Paint fourth part of wall.

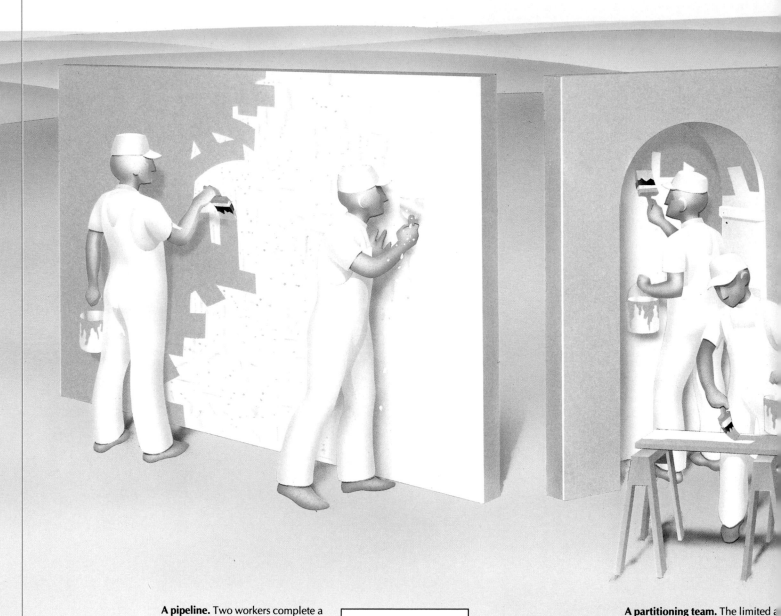

A pipeline. Two workers complete a wall in assembly-line fashion: The first scrapes from left to right, while the second paints far enough behind him that chips do not mar the wet surface. Since scraping takes longer than painting, the second worker can go no faster than the first. Similarly, processors may be linked in a pipeline to perform a series of tasks — such as those needed to fill a business order — that each depend on the one before.

```
PROGRAM 4:

PAINTER 1              PAINTER 2
Scrape first          Wait.
part of wall.

Scrape second         Paint first
part of wall.         part of wall.

Scrape third          Paint second
part of wall.         part of wall.

Scrape fourth         Paint third
part of wall.         part of wall.

                      Paint fourth
                      part of wall.
```

A partitioning team. The limited access afforded by a closet with shelv (*above*) means the painters must p tition the task: They remove the shelv paint them and the closet individu ly, then return the shelves to their ori nal positions. An analogous job parallel processors would be to sor master list by breaking it into subli of equal length, then sorting each o individually before merging the The time spent in assigning each sub to a processor is offset by the ti saved in sorting them simultaneous

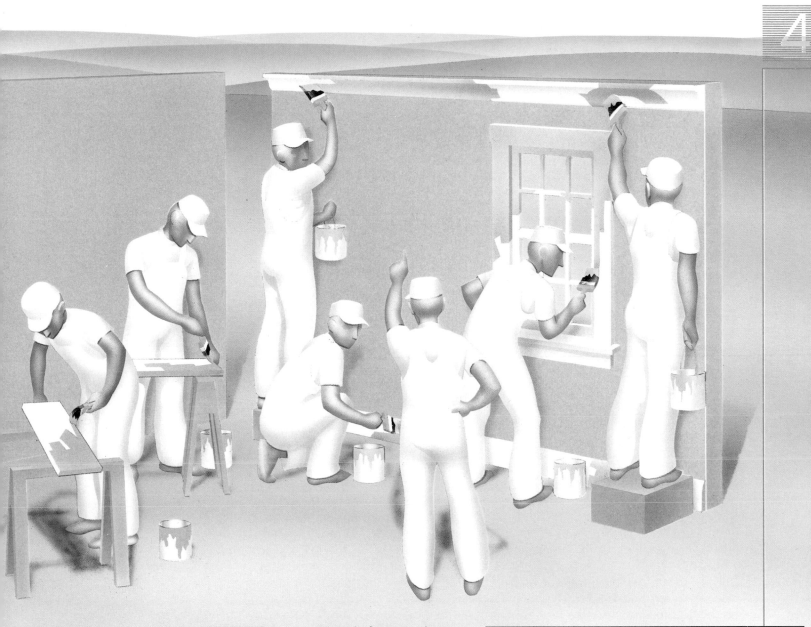

A supervised team. Synchronizing the stages of a job, a supervisor directs painting the wall and trim different colors. Before starting the trim, the painters must be told to clean their brushes, change paint colors and wait for the last worker to finish his portion of the wall. Similarly, parallel processors simulating the pattern of traffic in a neighborhood must be instructed to stop and exchange information whenever vehicles cross from one section of the neighborhood to another.

PROGRAM 5:

PAINTER 1	PAINTER 2	PAINTER 3	PAINTER 4
Remove and distribute three shelves.			
Paint inside of closet.	Paint shelf #1.	Paint shelf #2.	Paint shelf #3.
Wait until all shelves are painted.			
Replace shelves in closet.			

PROGRAM 6:

SUPERVISOR	PAINTER 1	PAINTER 2	PAINTER 3	PAINTER 4
Tell four painters to paint wall.				
	Paint first part of wall.	Paint second part of wall.	Paint third part of wall.	Paint fourth part of wall.
If any painter finishes early, tell him to wait until others are finished.				
Tell four painters to clean their brushes and change paint color.				
	Clean brush and change paint color.	Clean brush and change paint color.	Clean brush and change paint color.	Clean brush and change paint color.
Tell four painters to paint trim.				
	Paint first part of trim.	Paint second part of trim.	Paint third part of trim.	Paint fourth part of trim.

he did not hesitate to make it—even though in doing so he was bucking an oft-quoted Japanese proverb: "The nail that sticks up will get hammered down."

In 1985, Watanabe's efforts paid off, and NEC scored a major coup, becoming the first foreign supercomputer maker to install a machine on U.S. soil. The SX-2's buyer was the Houston Area Research Center (HARC), a consortium of four Texas universities. Acquisition of a supercomputer placed HARC among a handful of American academic institutions lucky enough to possess these coveted research tools. The group's choice of machine also landed it in the middle of a controversy. NEC was only one of several computer makers who bid for HARC's business: The rivals included Cray Research, Control Data's spin-off ETA Systems, IBM and Fujitsu. NEC offered by far the best deal for a demonstrably fast machine: At nine million dollars—some $13 million below the list price—the SX-2 cost roughly half the going rate for a comparable Cray or Cyber computer. The fire-sale price attracted the attention of the U.S. Department of Commerce's trade strike force, which began looking into the possibility that NEC was guilty

of unfair trade practices.

As it happened, a major part of the discount stemmed from an agreement that allowed NEC to have time-sharing access to the system. Olin Johnson, director of HARC's Computer Systems Applications Research Center, further justified the Center's choice by pointing out that NEC's machine—unlike its American rivals—came with considerable systems support and no fewer than 250 ready-to-use programs. So, despite their initial outcry, spurned American companies declined to file suit, and the government inquiry died quietly. Cray's Rollwagen was philosophical. "They made a proposal that would have been ridiculous for us to try to match," he said, shrugging off his company's loss of the HARC deal. Besides, he added, with the SX-2 installed in the U.S., American manufacturers would finally have a chance to evaluate firsthand one of the much-heralded Japanese machines. Said Rollwagen: "We have them out in the open where we want them."

The question uppermost in everyone's mind was whether Japan's intensive research effort had yielded significant architectural breakthroughs. The answer, on the whole, was no. Like its American counterparts, the SX-2 offered a combination of scalar and vector processing capabilities, by then the standard configuration of supercomputing. Tadashi Watanabe took particular pride in the innovative way those features were arranged. The scalar control processor was equipped with four arithmetic pipelines, the vector processor with four sets of four, or 16 in all. With some relief, American experts pointed out that no matter how fast the SX-2 was, its architecture was merely an elaboration of the same pipe-lining techniques (pages 58-59) that had been in use since the 1960s. Far from being the revolutionary new machine the computing world might have expected from the highly touted Superspeed project, the SX-2 wandered scarcely at all from the architectural camp of conventional supercomputers such as the Cray and Cyber machines.

By the mid-1980s, U.S. supercomputer designers—even that confirmed con-

A strand of wire 11.78 inches long represents the precise distance covered in one nanosecond — a billionth of a second — by an electrical pulse traveling at the speed of light. Pioneer programmer Grace Murray Hopper has used such pieces of wire since the 1940s to illustrate the time-consuming effect of the length of a computer's circuits.

servative, Seymour Cray—had begun to move away from the serial von Neumann machine, with its single processor and single memory, and toward parallelism. Vector processor pipelines such as those in the SX-2 represented an incorporation of parallel elements into essentially single-processor designs. Both the Cray-2 and the Cray X-MP/48, a 1984 version of the twin-processor Cray X-MP, contained four processing units. A new computer then on the drawing boards at ETA Systems was designed to contain eight.

Although the American manufacturers were first with multiprocessor designs, they were not alone for long. By the end of the decade the Japanese supercomputer builders NEC and Fujitsu announced plans to market supercomputers with more than one processor. Fujitsu augmented its VP-2600 supercomputer with a second processor to compete with the Cray Y-MP. Each processor was rated at a peak theoretical speed of four gigaflops, double that of the Y-MP. NEC offered still higher speeds with its SX-3, which came in several versions; the top-of-the-line Model 44 had four processors and was said to be capable of a peak performance of 22 gigaflops. NEC, Fujitsu and Hitachi also began offering UNIX for their supercomputers, an operating system favored by most programmers and available on all Cray machines.

These multiprocessor supercomputers of the late 1980s are classified by the industry as relatively "small-n" (for "small number" of processors) computers. The real challenge to traditional architecture comes from so-called massively parallel computers that would yoke together hundreds or thousands—eventually even millions—of processing elements to attack various parts of a problem simultaneously. The concept of massively parallel processing had been on the back burners of computer research for most of the preceding decade, ever since the 64-processor ILLIAC IV failed to become commercially viable *(page 34)*. ILLIAC IV had tantalized engineers with its potential for quantum gains in speed, but the machine foundered on the immense difficulties inherent in programming it and on the high cost of its components. With the advent of very-large-scale integration (VLSI) technology in the late 1970s, however, researchers—particularly those interested in making progress on the frontier of artificial intelligence—again grew interested in parallelism.

In creating a machine with parallel architecture, designers must answer several critical questions. First, how many processors are necessary? Depending on the type of problem a machine is intended to solve, the number may vary from a few dozen powerful units (the so-called large-grain approach) to thousands or millions of much less powerful units (the small-grain approach). For instance, the small-grain approach is well suited to problems that are easily broken into many parts, such as AI programs requiring the machine to retrieve information quickly from enormous data bases. Second, the more processors the machine contains, the more critical is the scheme by which they are linked to each other, and the way they are synchronized. Should each processor be able to communicate with every other one, or only with its nearest neighbors? Similar questions arise with respect to memory: Should each processor be connected to a small amount of distributed memory, or should they all share a single large memory? Finally, designers and software engineers must decide who should be responsible for dividing a problem into parts to run on the parallel machine. Programming is simplified if the computer is equipped with software that can perform this chore automatically, but chances are the resulting code will be inefficient. Leaving the job to the human programmer might make for greater efficiency, but—as ILLIAC IV proved—programming becomes much more difficult.

All of these problems are familiar to the researchers working on Japan's Fifth Generation project. Western visitors to Fifth Generation laboratories have reported that evidence of major breakthroughs was scarce. The Japanese "had some limited machines running in a very structured way," said an IBM official, "but the hard technical accomplishments I had expected to see weren't there." Another observer, well acquainted with the Fifth Generation's lavish promises, concurred: "Many things they bit off were very large-scale, complex projects that have really baffled Western researchers for years."

THE CEDAR ALTERNATIVE

In the United States, one leader in the study of how to program parallel processors efficiently is David Kuck, director of the Center for Supercomputing Research and Development at the University of Illinois. One of his former students, Cray X-MP designer Steve Chen, has described his erstwhile teacher as "the leading factor in pioneering supercomputers." An outspoken man who has been associated with the university since 1965, Kuck is one of today's most respected theorists in the field of parallel processing.

Looking back over supercomputer developments in recent years, Kuck sees two problems. In his opinion, designers like Seymour Cray clung to traditional von Neumann design long after its limitations were apparent. Second, few supercomputer companies have given enough thought to the user's potential difficulties in adapting applications to the superfast machines. "Companies build a machine and then think about the software," he once complained. "Or they don't think about it at all, and let the users worry about it. That's why nobody can make the machines run at their rated peak capacity."

Kuck and his associates at Illinois have tackled the problem by designing a multiprocessor supercomputer system, called Cedar, that addresses both hardware and software issues. They created innovative language compilers to make program development easier for the user by automatically arranging data and instructions to spread over a parallel system. In a further effort to make parallel supercomputers practical for ordinary users, Kuck and his crew came up with a software package, called Parafrase, that converts applications software originally written for a serial computer to a form usable on a parallel machine.

The Cedar system links clusters of processors to a shared, or global, memory. Each of the clusters consists of a modified Alliant FX/8 mini-supercomputer incorporating eight 64-bit floating-point processors, vector instructions and a UNIX operating system (software widely adapted for use in parallel processors). In addition to the global memory, each cluster has its own memory, as does each of the processors within the cluster. Kuck has pointed out that the performance of a supercomputer is usually limited by the size of its memory and the speed with which the processor (or processors) can gain access to data stored there. Cedar's triple-tiered memory hierarchy serves the dual purpose of speeding the flow of data through the machine and keeping down the overall cost of memory. Kuck accomplished this by employing small, fast memories (at a higher cost per bit) near the processors and larger, slower memories (with a lower cost per bit)

A New Architecture to Keep Data Flowing

Dataflow, a scheme for speeding up multiprocessor systems, represents a truly radical departure from traditional ways of executing instructions. Instead of relying on a centralized control element to run programs step by step *(pages 52-55)*, dataflow systems distribute control to the data itself: Each piece of information has a hand in activating processors as it moves through the system. Although conventional computers with multiple processors can whiz through a program by working on various parts of it concurrently, identifying all the opportunities for such parallel processing — and then coordinating processor action — is a major programming headache.

For example, elaborate sequencing instructions may be needed to ensure that an operation on a variable affected by other computations will be executed in the right order.

Dataflow relieves the programmer of these details: Instructions are processed only when relevant data is available, so independent operations run simultaneously and dependent ones cannot be invoked out of turn. A graphical language *(below, left)* that expresses the relationships among instructions lets programmers exploit dataflow's potential for maximizing concurrency and keeps processing going at top speed.

Programs written in this graphical language are then converted to the dataflow machine's own language. As shown in the simplified model below and on the next two pages, such machine-language programs consist of instruction packets and data tokens, each containing information *(represented here by various colors)* that matches data with instructions and directs results to their next destination.

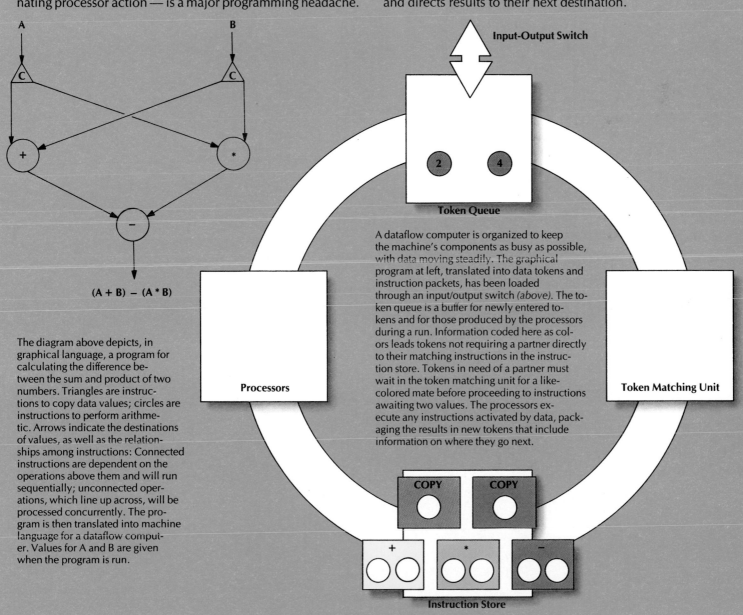

$$(A + B) - (A * B)$$

Input-Output Switch

Token Queue

Processors

Token Matching Unit

COPY   **COPY**

Instruction Store

The diagram above depicts, in graphical language, a program for calculating the difference between the sum and product of two numbers. Triangles are instructions to copy data values; circles are instructions to perform arithmetic. Arrows indicate the destinations of values, as well as the relationships among instructions: Connected instructions are dependent on the operations above them and will run sequentially; unconnected operations, which line up across, will be processed concurrently. The program is then translated into machine language for a dataflow computer. Values for A and B are given when the program is run.

A dataflow computer is organized to keep the machine's components as busy as possible, with data moving steadily. The graphical program at left, translated into data tokens and instruction packets, has been loaded through an input/output switch *(above)*. The token queue is a buffer for newly entered tokens and for those produced by the processors during a run. Information coded here as colors leads tokens not requiring a partner directly to their matching instructions in the instruction store. Tokens in need of a partner must wait in the token matching unit for a like-colored mate before proceeding to instructions awaiting two values. The processors execute any instructions activated by data, packaging the results in new tokens that include information on where they go next.

Tracking the Path of Data Tokens

The program active in this series of diagrams demonstrates how data in a dataflow system determines the timing of program execution. Instrumental in this process is the copy instruction, which supplies multiple copies of data values so that they can be used as soon as they are needed. Because these copies travel as independent data tokens that control their own processing, dataflow computers are able to keep their processors well-supplied with data.

In addition to the information that links them to their tokens, instruction packets also carry vital sequence coding that directs results to the next processing step. Thus, in the example shown here, the brown and purple copy instructions not only make copies of their tokens' values but also pass on information — the new colors green and yellow — that tells the copies to find like-colored partners and head for like-colored instructions.

Since more complex programs may call for the same instruction repeatedly, the original packet would normally stay in the instruction store, and a copy would be sent to the processors. For clarity, the instructions here are shown leaving the store after their tokens arrive.

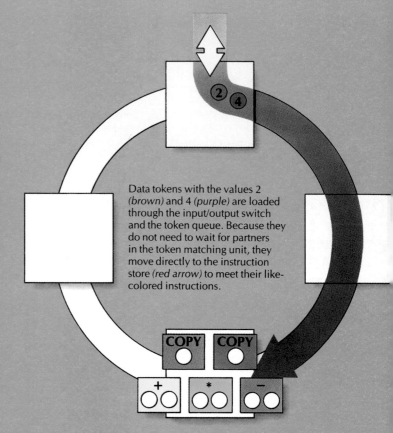

Data tokens with the values 2 (*brown*) and 4 (*purple*) are loaded through the input/output switch and the token queue. Because they do not need to wait for partners in the token matching unit, they move directly to the instruction store (*red arrow*) to meet their like-colored instructions.

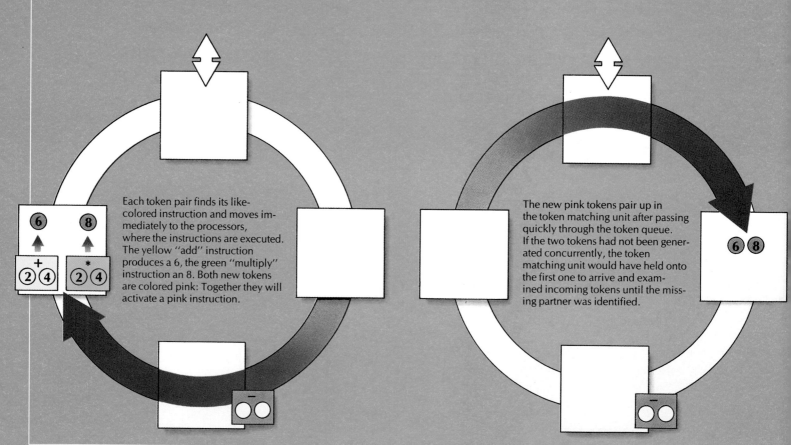

Each token pair finds its like-colored instruction and moves immediately to the processors, where the instructions are executed. The yellow "add" instruction produces a 6, the green "multiply" instruction an 8. Both new tokens are colored pink: Together they will activate a pink instruction.

The new pink tokens pair up in the token matching unit after passing quickly through the token queue. If the two tokens had not been generated concurrently, the token matching unit would have held onto the first one to arrive and examined incoming tokens until the missing partner was identified.

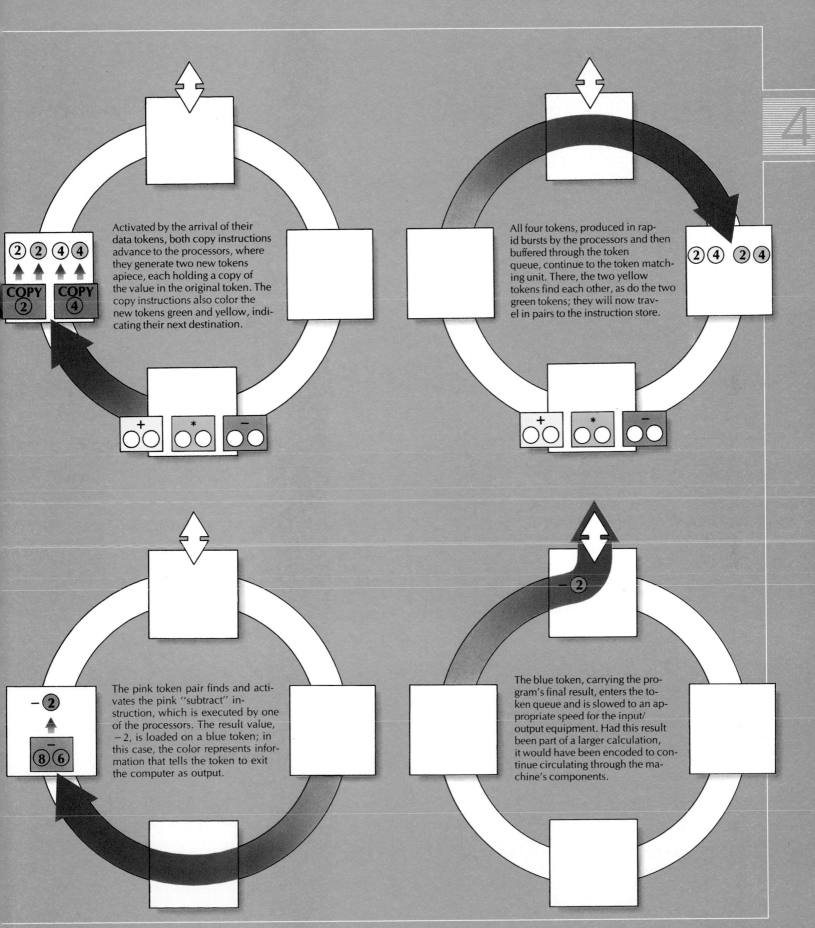

Activated by the arrival of their data tokens, both copy instructions advance to the processors, where they generate two new tokens apiece, each holding a copy of the value in the original token. The copy instructions also color the new tokens green and yellow, indicating their next destination.

All four tokens, produced in rapid bursts by the processors and then buffered through the token queue, continue to the token matching unit. There, the two yellow tokens find each other, as do the two green tokens; they will now travel in pairs to the instruction store.

The pink token pair finds and activates the pink "subtract" instruction, which is executed by one of the processors. The result value, −2, is loaded on a blue token; in this case, the color represents information that tells the token to exit the computer as output.

The blue token, carrying the program's final result, enters the token queue and is slowed to an appropriate speed for the input/output equipment. Had this result been part of a larger calculation, it would have been encoded to continue circulating through the machine's components.

farther away. "Blocks of information are moved from the slower level to faster levels of the hierarchy as needed," he wrote for one scientific journal. "A well-designed hierarchy has an effective access time near that of the fastest memories, and a cost per bit near that of the largest memories." The first Cedar system consisted of two clusters operating independently. Ultimately, Kuck plans for the system to incorporate 32 clusters, or 128 processors in all.

With 128 processors, Cedar is considered a relatively large-grain machine. Another in this category—and one of the first available commercially—is Intel's iPSC, a computer broadly based on work done over a period of about seven years by Charles Seitz, Geoffrey Fox and their colleagues at the California Institute of Technology. The Cal Tech machine, known as the Cosmic Cube, employs a so-called hypercube design: Sixty-four processors, each with the power of an IBM PC, are linked together to form a six-dimensional hypercube. (In two dimensions, four computers would form the corners of a square; in three dimensions, eight computers would link to form a normal cube, and so forth.) Each computer, or node, is wired directly to six of its neighbors. Each node works on a separate part of a problem, pausing as needed to receive new input or pass information on to other nodes. Messages traveling through a network of communications channels coordinate the separate computations.

The inventors of the Cosmic Cube proved the machine's mettle by tackling a problem in quantum chromodynamics: calculating the short- and long-range forces between subatomic particles called quarks. Crunching numbers at the rate of one billion arithmetic operations per hour, the computer took more than three months accumulated run-time to finish the job. Other researchers have since devised concurrent algorithms to allow the machine to handle calculations in such fields as high-energy physics, fluid mechanics and astrophysics, modeling problems as disparate as the movements of grains of sand and the birth of the universe. All of these calculations can be mapped in three or more dimensions, and not every problem is amenable to this treatment. But Seitz and Fox decided early on that the Cosmic Cube would be tailored to just this sort of scientific and engineering endeavor.

Intel's commercial version of the Cosmic Cube, which appeared in 1985, was also geared for the scientific market. "We want this to be the 'Access' machine," said Intel vice president Edward Slaughter in unveiling the iPSC, "the computer that people can get their hands on, where they can try things out and learn what can be done with parallel processing." The machine's 32 microprocessors were packaged in a sleek, four-foot-high silver tower resting on a two-foot-high base. Larger versions came with 64 and 128 processors, enabling the iPSC line to muster nearly half the power of a Cray-1 at a fraction of the cost. Two subsequent versions of the iPSC—the iPSC II and the iPSC 860—kept the 128-processor design but made it faster by replacing the original microprocessors with speedier chips as they became available.

Two approaches that explore the frontiers of parallel-processing architecture and programming are dataflow and reduction machines. Pioneered in the 1970s by M.I.T.'s Jack Dennis, dataflow architecture is language-based: The system is designed as a hardware interpreter for a specific base language, and programs to be run on the system must be expressed in that language. Dennis took this approach to get around the problem of adapting conventional (serial) software techniques to machines that employ ever greater degrees of parallelism. "The architects of supercomputers and multiprocessor systems have not addressed this challenge," Dennis wrote in 1979, "trusting that the 'software problem' can be successfully attacked by the 'software people.' This is fallacious."

The principle of the dataflow machine and its language (pages 99-101) is that there is no central controller issuing carefully orchestrated sequences of instructions. Rather, many processors are triggered by the arrival data from other processors: Using instructions stored in memory, each processor performs its assigned calculation and forwards the result to another processor, ensuring a constant flow of data through all the processors. In effect, the data controls the computation—automatically exploiting the concurrency of the architecture without special effort by the programmer. Such a machine seems most useful for evaluating simple expressions that evolve independent calculations on large streams of data—as are needed in some forms of process control, for instance, or in the control of robots.

Another attempt to simplify programming while increasing parallel execution is known as reduction architecture. In one machine, developed by Gyula Magó, a professor at the University of North Carolina in Chapel Hill, programs and data are, in effect, mixed together; the machine incorporates the results of each computation, continually rewriting a program and its data until no more computations are possible. In Magó's scheme, the machine is composed of two types of computing cells: T (for tree) cells carry out instructions and function as a routing network; L (for leaf) cells store parts of a program and handle processing related to managing that storage. The T cells are each permanently programmed to perform a limited repertory of tasks, such as addition or comparison. When the computer is fed a complex formula to evaluate, the cells are partitioned into subtrees, each designed to execute or reduce some part of the original formula. Following a "bottom up" approach, each T cell performs one part of the overall calculation and passes the result to another T cell higher up. Results can also move downward, to allow other T cells to complete their operations.

MAKING CONNECTIONS

While some dataflow machines have actually gone into operation (the DDP, or Distributed Data Processor, built by Austin-based Texas Instruments, was installed at the University of Southwestern Louisiana in 1978 and ran for half a decade), the reduction machine is still at the experimental stage. One of the handful of parallel computers to achieve more than experimental status is the Connection Machine, a massively parallel system with more than 64,000 processors. The Connection Machine, created by a young genius and entrepreneur named Daniel Hillis, made its debut in April 1986. Like Magó's reduction machine, the Connection Machine was designed to break problems down into smaller pieces—thousands of pieces—before operating on them simultaneously. In concept, Hillis' device was inspired by the human brain: It was originally intended for applications in artificial intelligence that require large bodies of information—the rules of a sophisticated expert system, for example—to be searched repeatedly and rapidly.

In an industry known for entrepreneurs who cut their teeth on computers, Hillis was a relative latecomer. When he entered M.I.T. in 1974, he had intended to study neuroscience because he considered the human brain "the most exciting mystery left in science." Somewhere along the line, one of his professors advised him: "If you want to learn how the brain works, study computers instead of medicine." Hillis began spending time in M.I.T.'s artificial intelligence lab, headed by AI pioneer Marvin Minksy. Eventually, he changed his major to electrical engineering and went on to earn a master's degree and a doctorate in the same field.

Even during his student days, Hillis was given to offbeat projects. In one memorable burst of ingenuity, he used 10,000 Tinkertoy pieces to build a computer that played tic-tac-toe (below, right). Further tinkering during his spare time at M.I.T. led to the creation of a robot turtle that could draw and a propeller-driven jump suit that allowed its wearer to walk on water.

But it was during his postgraduate years that Hillis began to apply his background in neuroscience to his work in computer engineering. Breaking completely with von Neumann architecture, Hillis embarked on a machine designed to mimic the neuronal activity of the human brain. The project that began as Hillis' Ph.D. thesis ultimately resulted in the Connection Machine, a three-dimensional architecture in which 65,536 processors can be connected as if they form a 16-dimensional cube (65,536 being the number two raised to the 16th power). Each processor, which has its own tiny memory bank, is connected to 16 others and is never more than 16 steps away from any other processor in the machine. The whole connection scheme is a network of 4,096 switching stations and 24,576 trunk lines—much like a miniature telephone system, in which each processor-memory element has its own telephone. Most important, all of these connections can be programmed and reprogrammed without touching the wiring, so that the machine can easily reconfigure the pattern of connections among the processors to suit the problem that is to be worked on.

The Connection Machine needs a front-end processor to feed it a serial stream of instructions. Thus, it is a single instruction/multiple data stream, or SIMD, computer that carries out single instructions on a large body of data. (Machines such as the Cray-2, Cray Y-MP and the Cosmic Cube, in contrast, are categorized as multiple instruction/multiple data stream, or MIMD, capable of operating on different instructions simultaneously.)

NURTURING A BREAKTHROUGH

In 1983, Hillis helped found Thinking Machines Corporation, a firm dedicated to producing a breakthrough computer, and continued work on his brainchild. DARPA, in keeping with the push to meet the challenge of Japan's Fifth Generation project, provided grants totaling $4.7 million for the research. In late 1985, more than a year ahead

Connection Machine designer Danny Hillis (below, left, in the plaid shirt) plays tic-tac-toe with one of his earlier creations, a primitive parallel processor made of Tinkertoys. Built in the late 1970s, the machine was intended to demonstrate that it would have been possible to build a computer in the 19th century: In place of electronic circuits, Hillis used string pulled tight by lead weights to activate wooden logic gates.

of schedule, the firm delivered a 65,536-processor machine to DARPA.

The following April, the first commercial version went to Perkin-Elmer, the world's leading maker of analytical instrumentation. Scaled down to 16,384 processors, the machine was installed at a Perkin-Elmer subsidiary, MRJ, Inc., in Oakton, Virginia. MRJ, which does contract work for NASA as well as for the Department of Defense, has put the Connection Machine to work on a variety of military problems. One that arises frequently pertains to aircraft: Given a destination and the position of enemy radar, what flight path should a pilot take to minimize the chance of being detected? In a classic use of the Connection Machine's distributed memory, each processor is assigned to represent a different point in space, speeding up by many orders of magnitude the mathematical calculations that must be made.

Later, at its public unveiling, the full-scale machine was put through its paces by its inventors, zipping through a series of trials at eyeblink speed. First, it took a mere 1/20 of a second to scan data files of 16,000 Reuters news stories and retrieve a particular article. Then it used another two seconds to turn the stereoscopic image of a hill, transmitted by a pair of TV cameras, into a detailed, two-dimensional contour map. The machine capped this performance with a three-minute finale during which it mapped out the ideal circuitry for a computer chip containing 4,000 transistors. Slated for use in such applications as AI research and image analysis (each processor can look at a different part of the image so that the machine, in effect, perceives the whole image at once, much as the eye does), the Connection Machine clearly pleased its financial backers: DARPA ordered two of Hillis' first six machines. "It has surpassed our expectations," said DARPA spokesperson Stephen Squires. "This made a lot of barriers go away—it will push back the frontiers of AI for many years to come."

Thinking Machines' fortunes continued to soar in the years that followed. By the end of the 1980s, the ambitious start-up had become a profitable firm with dozens of commercial customers, most with more than one Connection Machine. Some of the computers were assigned tasks usually allocated to conventional supercomputers. Mobil, for example, enlisted a Connection Machine in its search for underground oil, and Boeing used one to model airflow over the wings of a proposed plane. In other cases, the Connection Machine's superlative data-handling abilities suggested other applications, from the analysis of consumer buying patterns to the matching of DNA sequences in different proteins. One well-known customer, Dow Jones Company, used two Connection Machines to sort through its Dow Quest financial database, retrieving information for subscribers at a lightning pace.

ON THE CUSP OF A NEW ERA
Thinking Machines has moved on toward its next goal—a one-million-processor machine—and computer scientists and engineers worldwide are racing to bring their own multiprocessors to market. But the future is anyone's guess, although it is clear that the age of sequential computing has virtually drawn to a close. As early as 1983, at a conference of supercomputer designers and users held at Los Alamos Laboratory, Cray's John Rollwagen mused on the fundamental differences between serial and parallel processing. "I think that Seymour Cray and our industry have been building left brains," he said, speaking in terms of contem-

porary research that divides the twin hemispheres of the brain into complementary functions. "These are big, dumb, but fast machines that follow one step at a time. I think that we are on the threshold of exploring at least the idea of building right brains." Illinois's David Kuck certainly agrees. In terms of conventional computers, "we're at the end of our rope," he declared.

For purposes of finding the successor to the von Neumann machine, Kuck is placing his money on large-grain computer systems like the Cedar or the Cosmic Cube. But there are equally strong supporters of small-grain systems along the lines of the Connection Machine, as well as of new approaches such as those taken by the dataflow and reduction machines. (The Japanese, for their part, have produced a dataflow machine—the Sigma 1—that employs 256 processing elements and can hit 100 megaflops on scientific problems.)

David Shaw, a computer scientist who developed an experimental small-grain system similar to the Connection Machine, admits there are many issues still to be resolved. "It's clear to everybody that if you want to do a particular problem as fast as you can," he says, "it will be best done by a special-purpose machine. None of us is going to come up with a general-purpose machine that will do as well." But if the prize is for coming up with the most widely used architecture of the future, he adds, general-purpose is more useful than special-purpose. "It will be some new way of organizing computers that, although it isn't perfect, is good enough for people to adopt it for 90 percent of what they do." Rollwagen, looking to the future, seems to lean toward Shaw and Hillis' vision: "These massively parallel machines with new kinds of architecture and new kinds of software and algorithms perhaps can simulate how we make intuitive leaps."

Toward
Swifter
Switching

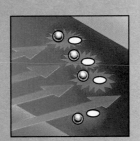

Of all the ways to accelerate a computer, perhaps none holds greater immediate promise than faster switching — increasing the rate at which a computer's electronic synapses are tripped from off to on, 0 to 1, negative to positive. Already, the switches of a supercomputer can function in less than a billionth of a second, enabling the computer to perform millions of operations in the time it takes an electric lamp to light. To computer engineers, however, even that pace seems ponderous. In pursuit of the ultimate computing velocity, they have devised an assortment of speedy switches — pictured on the following pages — that range from the viable to the visionary.

Switches form the foundation of modern computers. They hold the binary digits that represent information within the computer, and by opening and closing pathways they channel that information as well. In the complex web of a computer circuit, switches run by chain reaction, with the output of one forming the input to the next. The interactive weave means that switches may not be judged individually, by their swiftness alone: Computing speed also depends on the time required for an impulse to pass between them. If one switch is to trigger another within a billionth of a second, for instance, the two must be no more than about six inches apart.

But switch proximity is not sufficient to guarantee speed-up. For greater processing power, the switches themselves must be small enough for millions of them to fit into the confines of a computer chip. In such close quarters, however, the switches demand cooling as well; otherwise, the heat they generate would simply melt their circuitry.

The quest for faster, smaller and cooler switches has spurred computer engineers to explore a welter of new technologies and materials, some of which threaten to outmode the conventional silicon chip. Switches made from such exotic compounds as gallium arsenide offer higher performance, as do superconducting switches that require a cooling bath of liquid helium to sustain their breakneck speed. Nor is the prospect of abandoning electronic devices altogether so remote. Because optical switches are potentially the fastest of all, scientists are probing the possibilities of computing with beams of light — that is, with true light switches.

The Junction Diode: A Rudimentary Switch

The simplest computer switch is a junction diode *(opposite),* a device that makes use of two different regions of semiconductor material to conduct or block an electric current. Semiconductors are crystalline materials whose electrical resistance lies between that of good conductors, such as copper and aluminum, and that of insulators, such as rubber and glass. In their pure state, semiconductors behave more like insulators: Their electrons, tightly bound to their nuclei, are unable to respond to positive or negative voltages. But when small amounts of an impurity are incorporated — a process called doping — the semiconductors become excellent conductors.

Silicon — the most abundant chemical element after oxygen — has been the semiconductor of choice since the late 1950s. In a crystal of pure silicon *(below, left),* no electrons are free to carry current. When some of the silicon atoms are replaced by atoms of phosphorus *(below, center),* which have five outer electrons, the surplus electrons can respond to an applied voltage. Because electrons bear a negative charge, phosphorus-doped silicon is said to be an n-type semiconductor. The introduction of aluminum atoms *(below, right),* with three outer electrons, creates holes — areas of electron deficiency that carry a positive charge through the silicon as bubbles carry air through water. Butting an aluminum-doped, p-type region of silicon against its n-type counterpart forms a junction at the heart of the diode. The movement of electrons and holes across this junction abets current flow or aborts it.

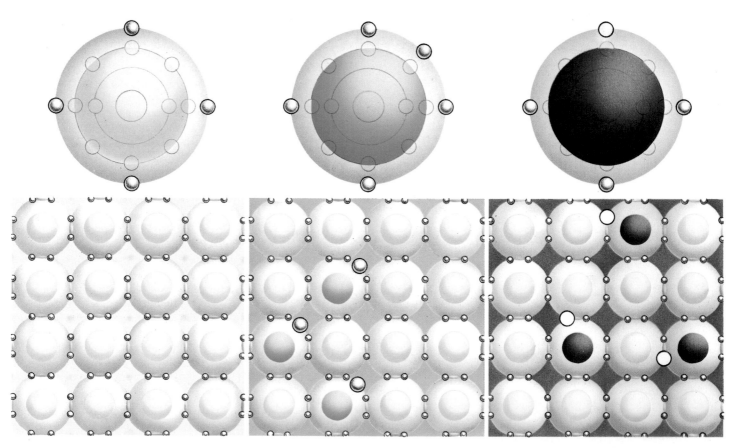

Pure silicon

In a crystal of pure silicon, each atom *(top)* shares the four electrons in its outer shell with the electrons of surrounding atoms, forming a tight lattice *(above)* in which no electrons are free to carry current.

N-type silicon

The extra electron in the outer shell of a phosphorus atom *(top)* creates an electron surplus in silicon that has been doped with phosphorus *(above).* The negatively charged electrons are now free to be attracted by a positive voltage or repelled by a negative one.

P-type silicon

The presence of only three electrons in the outer shell of an aluminum atom *(top)* produces holes in aluminum-doped silicon *(above).* Because the holes in effect carry a positive charge, they would move in the direction opposite that of electrons.

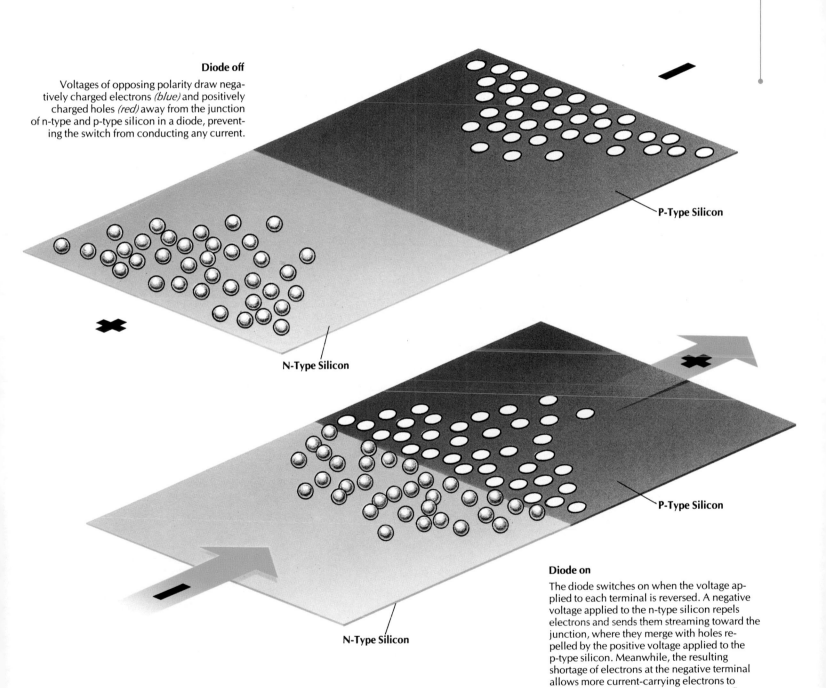

Diode off

Voltages of opposing polarity draw negatively charged electrons *(blue)* and positively charged holes *(red)* away from the junction of n-type and p-type silicon in a diode, preventing the switch from conducting any current.

P-Type Silicon

N-Type Silicon

P-Type Silicon

Diode on

The diode switches on when the voltage applied to each terminal is reversed. A negative voltage applied to the n-type silicon repels electrons and sends them streaming toward the junction, where they merge with holes repelled by the positive voltage applied to the p-type silicon. Meanwhile, the resulting shortage of electrons at the negative terminal allows more current-carrying electrons to enter there, and the current continues to flow.

N-Type Silicon

Two Types of Transistors

From mainframes to pocket calculators, virtually all of today's computers owe their speed to transistors — silicon switches that double as amplifiers, enabling a weak signal to control a much stronger one. The transistor family has grown two branches. In bipolar transistors *(below),* the current is carried by particles of both polarities — that is, by electrons and holes. The fastest bipolar switches operate in less than a billionth of a second, but to attain such speeds they devour relatively large amounts of power, all of which is given off as heat. As a result, no more than a few thousand

bipolar transistors can be mounted on a single silicon chip.

The other member of the transistor family is the MOSFET *(right),* an acronym that denotes the device's structure (metal-oxide semiconductor) as well as its function (field-effect transistor). The MOSFET is a unipolar switch: Current is carried by either electrons or holes, but not by both. Unique to the MOSFET is its gate electrode, a metal contact that controls the transistor current by creating an electric field. Because they require fewer layers than bipolar transistors, MOSFETs are easier to manufacture. And because they are also less power-hungry, they can be crammed onto a chip in large numbers; some MOSFET memory chips host more than a million transistors. There is a trade-off, however: Turning a MOSFET on and off requires moving a charge in and out of the metal gate, a relatively slow process compared with the switching of a bipolar transistor.

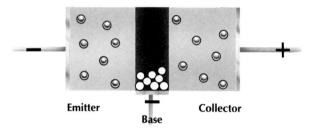

Emitter   Collector
        Base

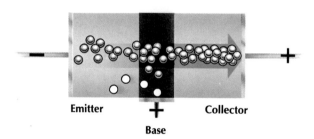

Emitter   +   Collector
        Base

Inside a bipolar transistor

In a bipolar transistor, a narrow boundary of p-type silicon called the base *(red)* governs the flow of current between the n-type emitter and collector *(blue).* The strong positive voltage at the collector attracts the negatively charged electrons in the emitter, but a small negative voltage at the base halts the current flow *(left, top).* A small positive voltage at the base removes the obstacle, allowing holes to course into the emitter and electrons to flow into the collector *(left, bottom).* As electrons surge through the base, the strength of the collector's positive charge lets only a few of them stray toward the base electrode.

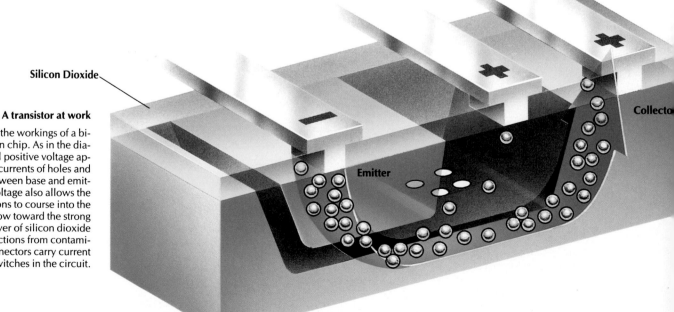

A transistor at work

A cross section reveals the workings of a bipolar transistor in a silicon chip. As in the diagram above, a small positive voltage applied to the base *(red)* sets currents of holes and electrons in motion between base and emitter. The small positive voltage also allows the main body of electrons to course into the collector, where they flow toward the strong positive terminal. A layer of silicon dioxide shields the transistor's junctions from contamination; the metal connectors carry current to and from other switches in the circuit.

Silicon Dioxide

Emitter

Collector

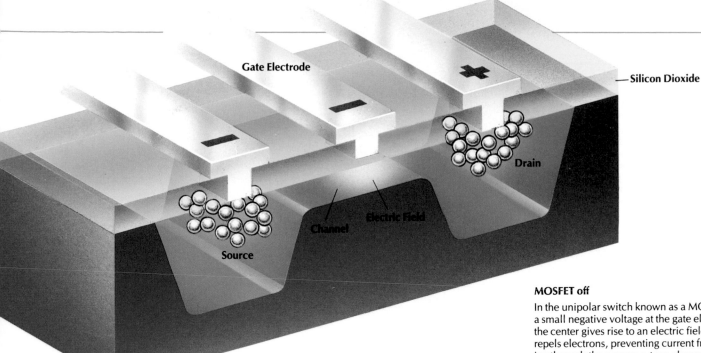

Gate Electrode

— **Silicon Dioxide**

Drain

Electric Field

Channel

Source

MOSFET off

In the unipolar switch known as a MOSFET, a small negative voltage at the gate electrode in the center gives rise to an electric field that repels electrons, preventing current from flowing through the narrow n-type channel and keeping the device turned off. Three regions in the n-type silicon — a pair of deep wells called the source and the drain, linked by the shallow sluicelike channel — correspond to the emitter, collector and base of a bipolar transistor *(opposite page)*. Metal conductors make contact with the source and the drain, but a thin layer of silicon dioxide separates the gate electrode from the channel.

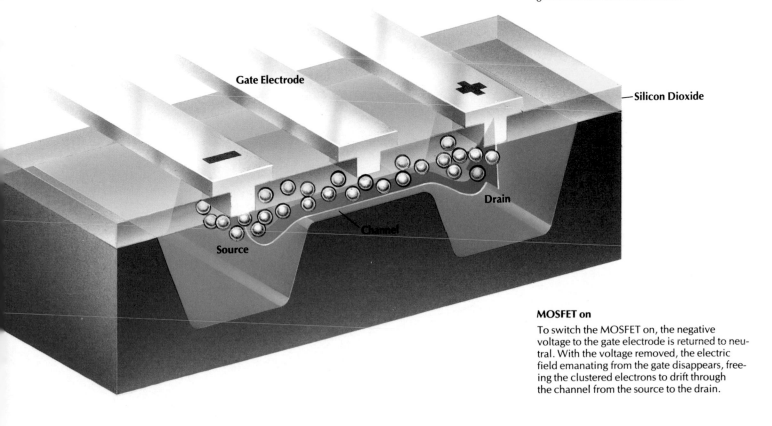

Gate Electrode

— **Silicon Dioxide**

Drain

Channel

Source

MOSFET on

To switch the MOSFET on, the negative voltage to the gate electrode is returned to neutral. With the voltage removed, the electric field emanating from the gate disappears, freeing the clustered electrons to drift through the channel from the source to the drain.

A High-Performance Semiconductor

The race for maximum switching speed has inspired scientists to fabricate a wide range of new semiconductors by combining chemical elements in ways not found in nature. Devices built from some of these exotic compounds switch on and off in as little as six trillionths of a second, far outstripping their speediest silicon-based rivals.

The synthetic semiconductor that enjoys the widest use is gallium arsenide, or GaAs, in which the quirky metal gallium is wedded to the poison arsenic. Brittle at low temperatures, gallium has such a low melting point that it turns liquid in the hand. Despite the odd behavior and sinister reputation of its respective components, GaAs stands up well to heat and op-

erates at low voltage, yielding a high-speed transistor that needs little cooling.

These desirable properties are offset, however, by a certain inconvenience in manufacturing. Brittle GaAs wafers demand special handling lest they shatter. And because gallium arsenide forms a powdery oxide, another material must be used to protect the surface of the device. Silicon dioxide can serve as a covering, but special measures must be taken to ensure that metal contacts joined to the GaAs conduct electricity properly.

More complex compounds that enhance the swiftness of GaAs portend still greater speed. In the layer-cake assembly at right, engineers have paired GaAs with its cousin, aluminum gallium arsenide (AlGaAs). In this scheme, a doped region supplies an abundance of current-carrying (or conduction) electrons, while an undoped region directly below provides a clear path for their passage. The result is a switch capable of turning on and off 230 billion times a second.

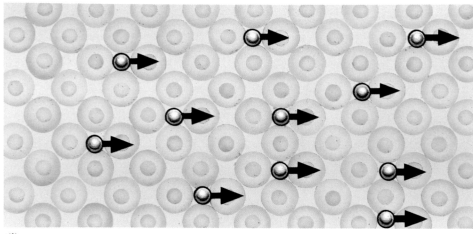

Silicon

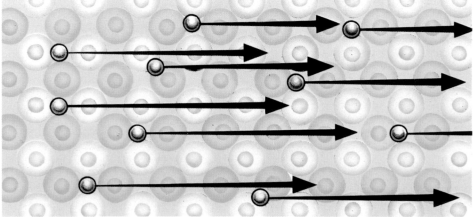

Gallium Arsenide (GaAs)

A fast track

Conduction electrons move more slowly through silicon *(left, top)* than through gallium arsenide *(bottom)*. In both crystals, the negatively charged electrons float in a sea of positive atomic charges like corks bobbing in water. Because of differences in the subatomic make-up of the two elements, however, the GaAs electrons are lighter and easier to propel. Thus the GaAs electrons accelerate more readily — and reach a higher top speed — in response to a given voltage.

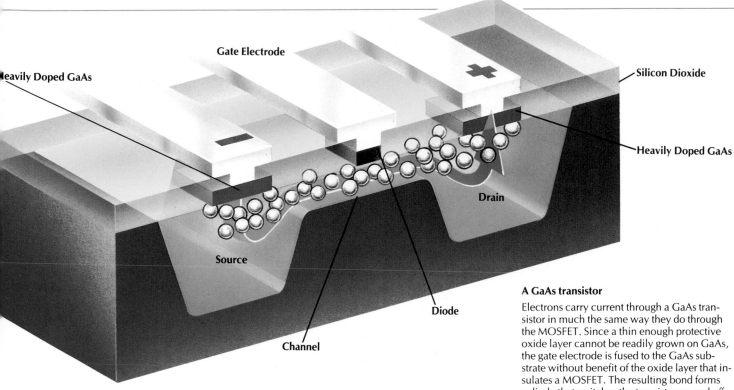

Gate Electrode

Heavily Doped GaAs

Silicon Dioxide

Heavily Doped GaAs

Drain

Source

Diode

Channel

A GaAs transistor

Electrons carry current through a GaAs transistor in much the same way they do through the MOSFET. Since a thin enough protective oxide layer cannot be readily grown on GaAs, the gate electrode is fused to the GaAs substrate without benefit of the oxide layer that insulates a MOSFET. The resulting bond forms a diode that switches the transistor on and off according to the voltage received at the gate electrode: As in a MOSFET, the lack of voltage allows current to pass because the diode emits no disruptive electric field. Heavily doped GaAs regions *(purple)* beneath the electrodes at the source and the drain prevent the formation of diode barriers that would interfere with normal conduction.

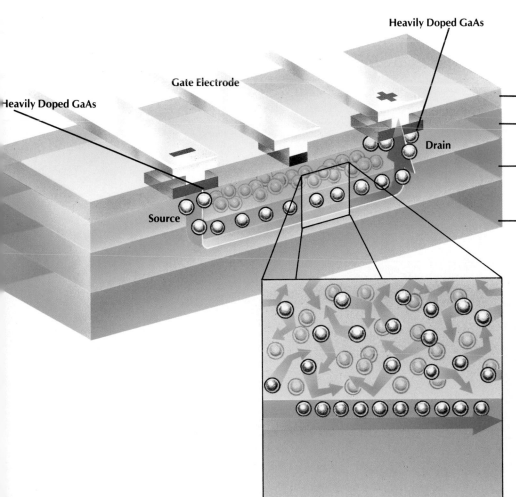

Heavily Doped GaAs

Gate Electrode

Heavily Doped GaAs

Silicon Dioxide

N-Type AlGaAs

Drain

Undoped GaAs

Source

GaAs Substrate

A switch with a passing lane

In the semiconductor switch called a high-electron-mobility transistor, or HEMT, conduction electrons arising in a doped layer of n-type aluminum gallium arsenide *(blue)* are drawn from left to right by a positive voltage at the drain and allowed to pass by the absence of a voltage at the gate. Slowed by collisions with atoms in the congested AlGaAs *(inset)*, the conduction electrons seek an open road in the undoped layer of gallium arsenide *(green)* directly below. There, unimpeded by any dopant atoms, the electrons flow to their rendezvous with the drain. GaAs substrate forms the transistor's foundation.

113

Superconductors for Supercomputing

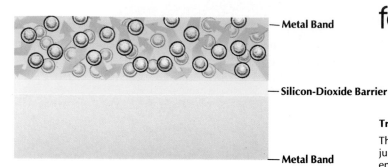

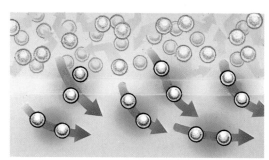

— Metal Band

— Silicon-Dioxide Barrier

— Metal Band

Traveling in tandem

The silicon-dioxide barrier in a Josephson junction superconductor switch is just thick enough to prevent individual electrons from traveling between two metal bands *(left, top)* but ineffective against pairs of electrons *(left, bottom).* Electron pairing occurs when the switch is immersed in a supercooled environment, which keeps thermal vibrations from breaking the pairs apart. In this situation, only the presence of a magnetic field *(below)* can disrupt them.

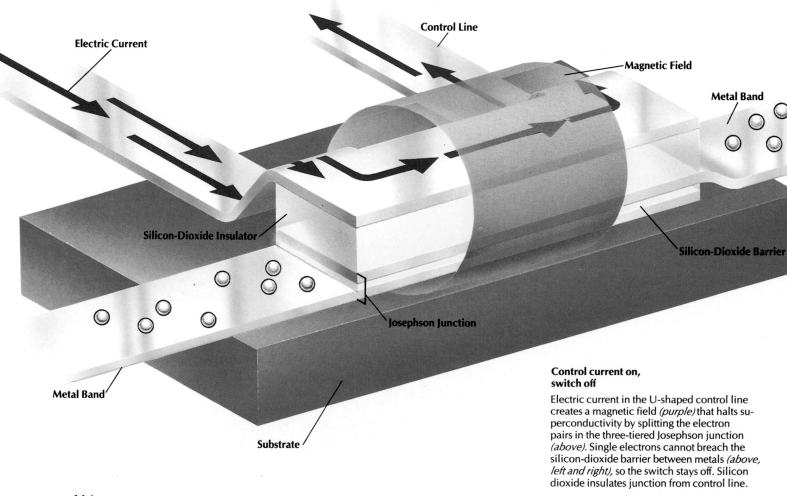

Electric Current

Control Line

Magnetic Field

Metal Band

Silicon-Dioxide Insulator

Silicon-Dioxide Barrier

Josephson Junction

Metal Band

Substrate

Control current on, switch off

Electric current in the U-shaped control line creates a magnetic field *(purple)* that halts superconductivity by splitting the electron pairs in the three-tiered Josephson junction *(above).* Single electrons cannot breach the silicon-dioxide barrier between metals *(above, left and right),* so the switch stays off. Silicon dioxide insulates junction from control line.

Electrical resistance and other factors—such as the tendency of electrons to collide with atoms in doped material *(page 113)*—account for the energy that is consumed by conventional semiconductor switches. The absence of these inhibiting mechanisms in a superconductor allows for high-speed switching with virtually no power consumption. Superconductivity is an effect peculiar to certain metals, such as lead or niobium, when they are cooled to below a specific temperature, often to a few degrees above absolute zero, or 273° C. below the freezing point of water. All metals, including superconductors, gradually grow more conductive as they are cooled. But as a superconductor's temperature falls, electrical resistance drops abruptly to nothing, inaugurating a state of conductivity that allows current to flow virtually forever. Such flow is called—aptly enough—supercurrent.

An entire superconducting computer, with millions of switches, might consume only a few watts of electricity— roughly the amount needed to run a flashlight. To achieve these energy savings, however, computers that employ superconductor switches must be cooled to the critical temperature, a process that may require submergence in a bath of liquid helium. Such cumbersome measures could one day be eliminated by the use of new superconductors, discovered during the late 1980s, that function at temperatures as high as 125° C. above absolute zero.

The superconductor switches that have drawn the greatest scrutiny are Josephson junctions *(below),* in which two metal electrodes sandwich an oxide insulator. Although the insulating layer is only a few dozen atoms thick, it blocks a standard current carried by individual electrons. A supercurrent, however, is transported through the switch by pairs of electrons; because their combined diameter is larger than the thickness of the insulating barrier, the pairs tunnel through.

A superconductor switch is normally on. It is turned off by sending a voltage through a superimposed control line, which generates a magnetic field that stymies the supercurrent.

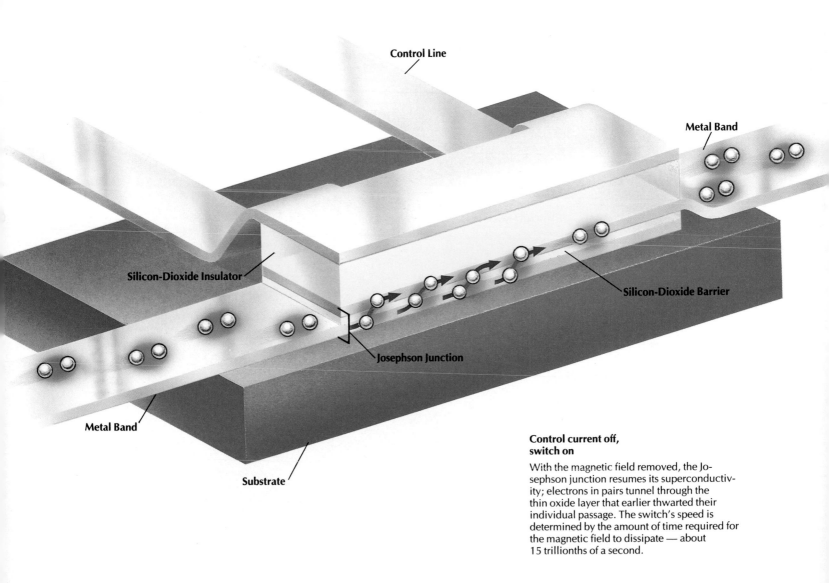

Control Line

Metal Band

Silicon-Dioxide Insulator

Silicon-Dioxide Barrier

Josephson Junction

Metal Band

Substrate

Control current off, switch on

With the magnetic field removed, the Josephson junction resumes its superconductivity; electrons in pairs tunnel through the thin oxide layer that earlier thwarted their individual passage. The switch's speed is determined by the amount of time required for the magnetic field to dissipate — about 15 trillionths of a second.

An Optical Alternative

A constant in the evolution of computer-switch technology from vacuum tube to integrated circuit has been the switch's function as an electronic device — one whose job is to direct a flow of electrons. An embryonic technology called optical computing makes a radical departure from that premise, triggering switches with photons — the component particles of light — rather than with electrons. The focus of photonic technology — indeed, the key to building an optical computer — is the optical switch, whose task is to block or transmit a beam of light.

Light waves are potentially the ultimate computing medi-

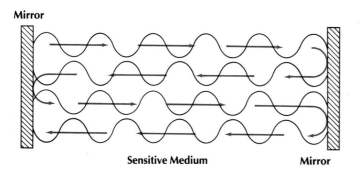

Mirror

Sensitive Medium　　　　**Mirror**

Beam blocked

In the illustration below, the sensitive medium of an optical switch *(purple),* bracketed by two parallel mirrors, denies passage to a faint beam of light issuing from the laser at left. The paired mirrors form an optical echo chamber, or cavity, in which trapped light waves carom back and forth, as in the diagram at left. The distance between the mirrors is such that the peaks of waves moving left to right align with the troughs of waves traveling in the opposite direction. In effect, each wave is canceled out by its mirror image.

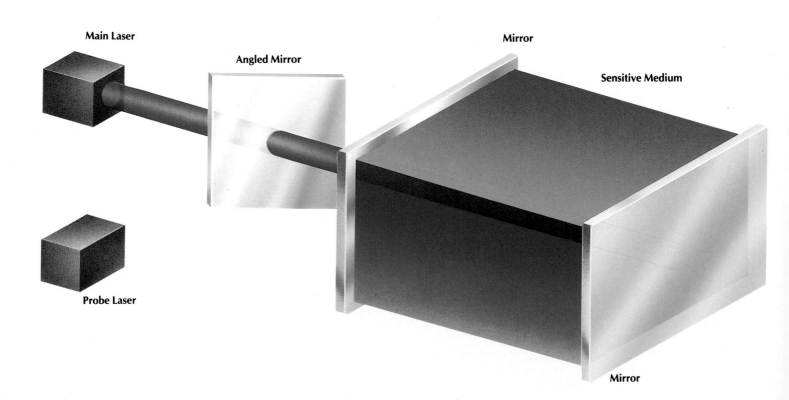

Main Laser

Angled Mirror

Mirror

Sensitive Medium

Probe Laser

Mirror

um, for nothing travels faster than light. Although the construction of optical switches remains a young art, already switching times rivaling those of the best gallium-arsenide transistors have been attained. The theoretical speed limit is higher still: Light-powered devices may someday operate in a few femtoseconds. (One femtosecond equals one thousandth of a millionth of a millionth of a second.)

A severe—perhaps prohibitive—liability of computing with light is power consumption. An optical switch that works a thousand times faster than a transistor may also require a thousand times more power and emit a thousand times as

much heat. To make optical computing a reality, switches that run by light must be made smaller, cooler and more efficient.

Pictured on these pages is one approach to building an optical switch. At the core of the device lies a substance — in some cases sodium vapor, in most cases a semiconductor such as indium phosphide — that allows the waves of a bright laser beam to travel through it slightly faster than those of a dim beam can travel. Two opposing mirrors translate this slight difference in speed into a dramatic difference in transparency, causing the switch to block a faint beam but let a bright one pass.

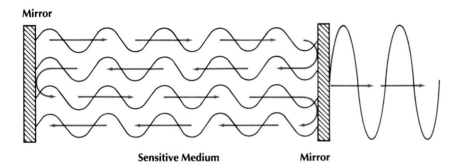

Mirror

Sensitive Medium   **Mirror**

Beam transmitted

The switch turns on when light from a second laser, called a probe, augments the first beam by means of an angled mirror. The intensity of the combined beam prompts a slight shift in the optical properties of the sensitive medium. As the diagram at left shows, the length of the optical cavity remains unchanged, but fewer waves fit between the mirrors. Peaks align with peaks and troughs with troughs, allowing the waves to reinforce one another and send the beam on its way.

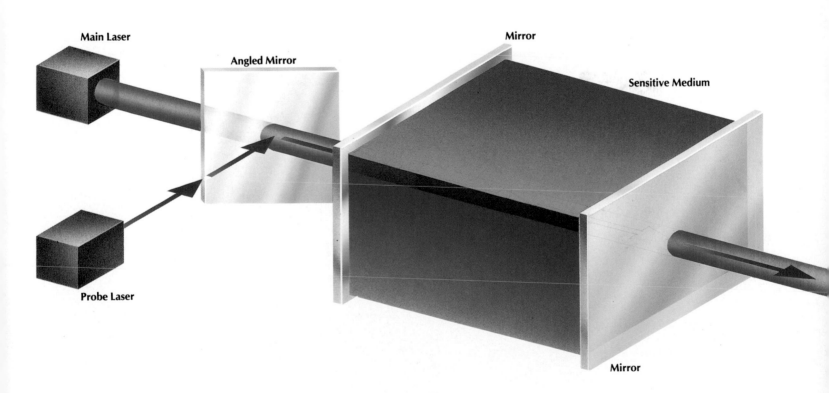

Main Laser

Angled Mirror

Mirror

Sensitive Medium

Probe Laser

Mirror

A Superlattice for Light Control

With optical properties as intriguing as their electronic ones, certain semiconductors offer an ideal medium for the "light switches" that may power the first optical computer. One such device, shown here, exploits the tendency of electrons and holes in a semiconductor to form light-absorbing duos called excitons. Although electrical connections to a power source are required to adjust, or tune, the light-absorbing frequency of the excitons, beams of light turn the switch off and on; the beams also constitute the transmitted signal. The

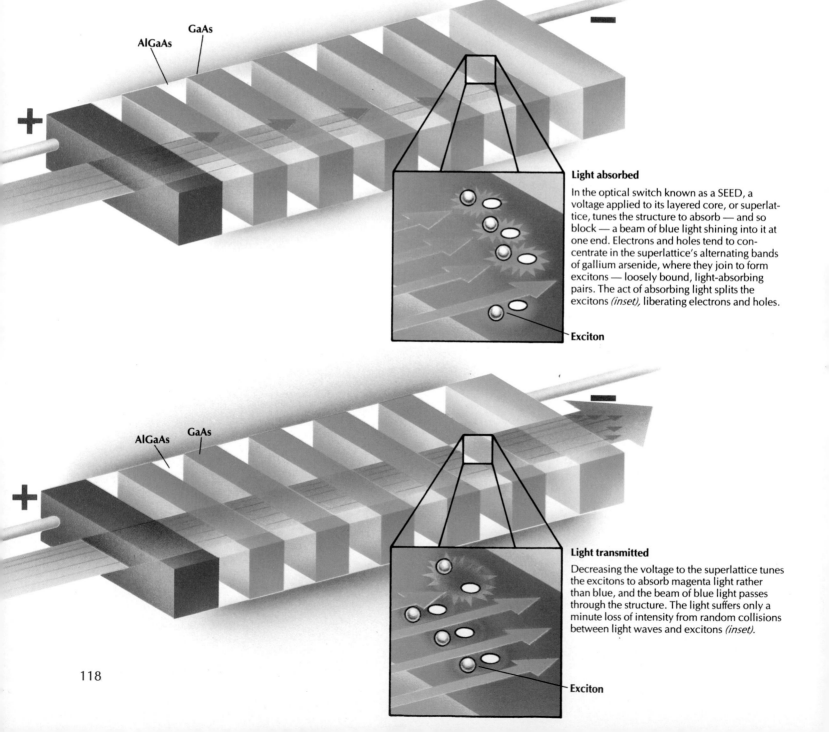

Light absorbed

In the optical switch known as a SEED, a voltage applied to its layered core, or superlattice, tunes the structure to absorb — and so block — a beam of blue light shining into it at one end. Electrons and holes tend to concentrate in the superlattice's alternating bands of gallium arsenide, where they join to form excitons — loosely bound, light-absorbing pairs. The act of absorbing light splits the excitons (inset), liberating electrons and holes.

Light transmitted

Decreasing the voltage to the superlattice tunes the excitons to absorb magenta light rather than blue, and the beam of blue light passes through the structure. The light suffers only a minute loss of intensity from random collisions between light waves and excitons (inset).

switch is called a self-electro-optic-effect device, or SEED, indicating that the light triggers electronic events, which in turn dictate whether the light is absorbed or transmitted.

The SEED's active element epitomizes the chipmaker's artistry: It is a superlattice *(opposite)* made up of 100 or more alternating layers of gallium arsenide (GaAs) and aluminum gallium arsenide (AlGaAs), each only a dozen atoms thick. The superlattice is a discriminating structure, absorbing certain wavelengths of light but allowing others to traverse it.

Which color will pass — and which will be intercepted — depends on the voltage applied to the ends of the superlattice.

In its most refined variation *(below),* the SEED features two stacked diodes, each containing a superlattice. The SEED remains off in the presence of a magenta control beam, which blocks the passage of the blue signal beam by tuning the lower diode to absorb light in the blue range of the color spectrum. Only in the control beam's absence can the blue beam pass through.

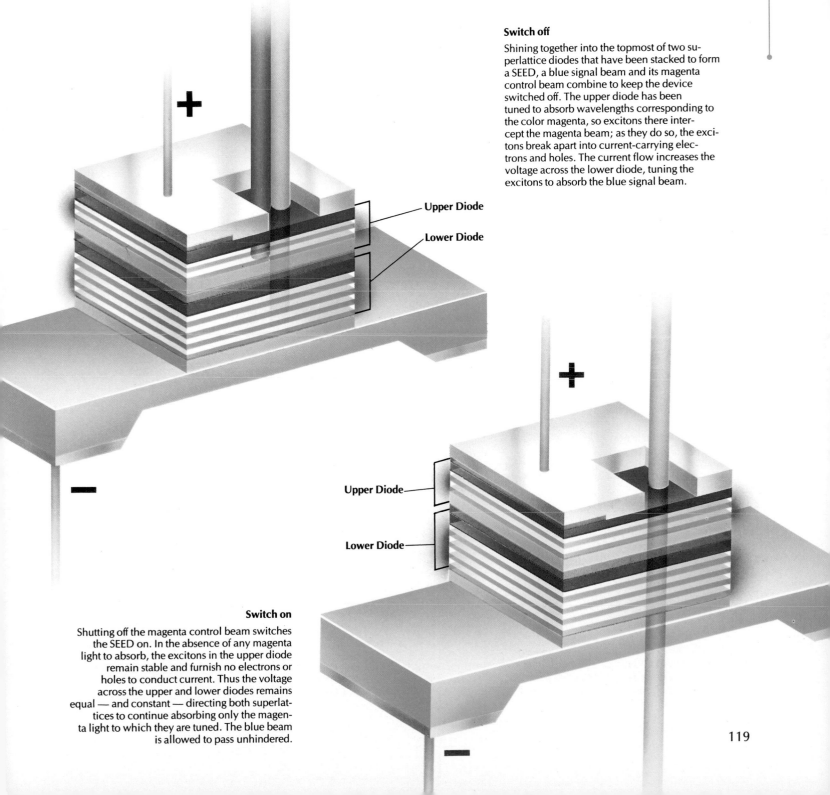

Upper Diode

Lower Diode

Switch off

Shining together into the topmost of two superlattice diodes that have been stacked to form a SEED, a blue signal beam and its magenta control beam combine to keep the device switched off. The upper diode has been tuned to absorb wavelengths corresponding to the color magenta, so excitons there intercept the magenta beam; as they do so, the excitons break apart into current-carrying electrons and holes. The current flow increases the voltage across the lower diode, tuning the excitons to absorb the blue signal beam.

Upper Diode

Lower Diode

Switch on

Shutting off the magenta control beam switches the SEED on. In the absence of any magenta light to absorb, the excitons in the upper diode remain stable and furnish no electrons or holes to conduct current. Thus the voltage across the upper and lower diodes remains equal — and constant — directing both superlattices to continue absorbing only the magenta light to which they are tuned. The blue beam is allowed to pass unhindered.

119

Glossary

Absolute zero: a hypothetical temperature characterized by complete absence of heat and equivalent to approximately $-273°$ C., or -459.7 F.

Algorithm: a step-by-step procedure for solving a problem.

Aluminum gallium arsenide (AlGaAs): a synthetic semiconductor, often paired with gallium arsenide in the formation of high-speed transistors.

Architecture: the design of a computer system, including both its hardware configuration and its software strategies for handling data and running programs. *See also* Von Neumann architecture.

Array processing: a processing technique in which a single control unit directs the activities of a group of processors, commanding them to perform the same operation simultaneously on different sets of data. *See also* Parallel processing.

Asynchronous execution: the running of multiple programs or parts of a program in which several processors work concurrently, without reference to one another's results.

Base: in a bipolar transistor, a narrow boundary of semiconductor material that permits or prevents a flow of current across it.

Batch processing: a processing method in which entire programs are loaded into the computer and executed one at a time.

Binary notation: a number system that uses two as its base and expresses numbers as combinations of zeros and ones. Information in a digital computer is processed and stored in binary form.

Binary tree architecture: a hardware design incorporating many layers of processors, beginning with a conventional serial processor that branches into two processing elements, each connected in turn to two more processors.

Bipolar transistor: a semiconductor switch in which current is carried both by electrons and by holes.

Bit: the smallest unit of information in a digital computer, represented by a single zero or one. The word "bit" is a contraction of "binary digit."

Buffer: a type of memory that temporarily holds data being transferred within a computer or from one computer device to another; buffers regulate rates of fast-moving data from supercomputers, for example, for less speedy peripheral equipment.

Bus: a communications channel that transmits information between parts of a computer or computer system; one of the three main components, along with the central processing unit (CPU) and memory, of a conventional von Neumann computer.

Byte: a series of bits, usually eight, treated as a unit for computation or storage.

Cache: a high-speed intermediate memory unit between main memory and the CPU that accelerates the fetching of data and instructions.

Central processing unit (CPU): the part of a conventional computer that interprets and executes instructions, as well as requesting the transfer of data to and from external sources; it is composed of a processor, a control unit and a small amount of memory.

Charge carriers: the electrons or holes that carry current through a semiconductor switch.

Clock: a device, usually based on a quartz crystal, whose regular pulses coordinate a computer's operations; each pulse corresponds to one phase of a computer's instruction cycle.

Collector: in a bipolar transistor, the region of semiconductor material that attracts current emanating from the emitter.

Computational chemistry: the study of the behavior of molecular, atomic or subatomic particles through computer manipulation of mathematical equations representing those particles.

Computationally intensive: pertaining to problems that require billions of mathematical calculations.

Concentrator: a support computer in a supercomputer center that manages files and buffers high-speed supercomputer data for slower-working peripheral devices.

Concurrency: the simultaneous execution of different parts of a program. *See also* Parallel processing.

Conduction electrons: electrons that carry current.

Contention overhead: in multiple-processor systems, delays caused when several processors vie for a single resource, such as a piece of data stored in main memory.

Control unit: the circuitry within a computer that manages the flow of processing. In conventional computers, the control unit is part of the CPU and directs activity in a step-by-step sequence known as the instruction cycle; in parallel-processing computers, one or more control units govern multiple processors.

Coprocessor: a subsidiary processor, controlled by the main processor, designed to perform specific tasks much faster than a general-purpose processor.

Core memory: a type of computer memory that stores information magnetically on tiny metallic rings.

Dataflow processing: a parallel-processing technique in which data travels through the computer as packages encoded with information that controls the execution of the program; individual packages activate processors to work concurrently or in sequence, as the data allows.

Data token: in dataflow processing, an individual package of data that contains a data value and encoded information directing the token to unite with a matching instruction packet; the data-instruction pair then proceeds immediately to one of the computer's processors to be executed.

Depth migration: a data-processing technique, used in seismic imaging, that compensates for distortions caused when reflected sonic waves travel through overlying rock.

Digital computer: any computer that operates on data expressed in discrete form, such as the ones and zeros of binary notation.

Disk: a round plate, generally made of plastic or metal with a magnetic coating, used for storing data.

Doping: introducing impurities into a semiconductor to enhance its conductivity.

Drain: in certain computer switches, the area toward which current flows when the switch is turned on; equivalent to the collector in a bipolar transistor.

DRAM (dynamic random-access memory) chip: an integrated circuit that serves as a temporary memory for program data. Although DRAM chips can store more information than any other type of memory chip, their circuits preserve data for only a short time, so the data must be continually refreshed, or rewritten onto the chip.

Emitter: in a bipolar transistor, the region of semiconductor material that supplies current-carrying electrons or holes.

Excitons: light-absorbing pairs of electrons and holes used to control the operation of optical switches.

Exponent: the power to which a base number is raised, as in 10^2 or 2^{-3}. In floating-point notation, the size of the exponent determines the placement of the decimal point in the mantissa; positive exponents move the decimal point to the left, negative exponents move the decimal point to the right.

Fetch instruction: the first phase of a typical instruction cycle, in which the control unit retrieves a program instruction from memory and loads it into the CPU.

Finite-element analysis: a computer technique that first divides a physical object into many smaller geometric shapes, or elements, then calculates how forces affect each element and how the elements affect one another.

Floating-point notation: a method of expressing numbers as the product of a fraction, or mantissa, and a base number raised to a certain power; so named because the decimal point moves, or floats, depending on the size of the exponent: For instance, 93,000,000 can become either $.93 \times 10^8$ or $.093 \times 10^9$. Floating-point notation allows supercomputers to work with very large and very small figures by reducing the number of digits needed to represent them.

Flops: floating-point operations per second; used as a measurement of processing speed in supercomputers.

Functional unit: a subdivision of processor circuitry that can perform specific operations, such as addition or multiplication; processors partitioned into functional units can perform two or more calculations simultaneously.

Gallium arsenide (GaAs): a synthetic semiconductor used in the construction of high-speed transistors and integrated circuits; valued for its low power consumption and ability to withstand heat.

Gate electrode: a metal contact that controls transistor current by creating an electric field.

Gateway computer: a support computer in a supercomputer center that performs security checks and protocol matching on incoming programs from external sources.

General circulation model (GCM): a mathematical representation of the earth's atmosphere and oceans, which is used in the study of weather patterns.

Gigaflops: one billion floating-point operations per second.

Global memory: the shared central memory of a multiple-processor system, as opposed to the local memory of individual processors.

Graphical language: a programming language often used for data-flow computers that outlines the relationships between program instructions, readily identifying opportunities for parallel processing.

High-electron-mobility transistor (HEMT): a semiconductor switch that provides a swift passage for current-carrying electrons through a layer of undoped semiconductor material.

Hole: an area of electron deficiency that acts as a positive-charge carrier.

Input/output controller: a specialized processor or computer that transfers data to and from external devices.

Instruction: an order in elementary machine-language specifying an operation to be carried out by the computer; a set of instructions forms a program.

Instruction cycle: the series of activities a computer performs in order to read an instruction from memory, decode it, execute it and prepare for the next instruction.

Instruction look-ahead: a computing method that allows for the partial decoding of imminent instructions in order to speed up processing.

Instruction packet: in dataflow processing, a package containing a particular instruction and encoded information that identifies matching data tokens. Once instruction and data are united, the packet moves to processing to be executed.

Instruction store: in a dataflow computer, a type of memory that stores a program's instruction packets; the original packets remain in the store, and copies are forwarded to processing when the appropriate data tokens arrive.

Integrated circuit: an electronic circuit made up of thousands of transistors and other electronic components, all formed on a single piece of semiconductor material; also known as a chip or a microchip.

Josephson junction: the heart of a superconductor switch, consisting of two metal electrodes separated by a thin layer of insulation, with a magnetic field controlling the flow of electrons across the insulation barrier. Josephson junctions operate at high speed, but they can function only at temperatures very close to absolute zero.

Junction diode: a simple computer switch composed of two regions of semiconductor material abutting each other; the switch is turned on or off by the presence or absence of a flow of electrons and holes across the junction.

Kernel: a small, self-contained portion of a more complex program.

Liquid-immersion cooling: a method of cooling computer components by bathing them in a liquid refrigerant.

Local area network (LAN): a computer system that links computers, computer workstations, printers and other peripheral devices in a network for transmitting data between offices in a building, for example, or between buildings situated near one another. Local area networks can be connected to supercomputer centers to provide ready access to a center's powerful machines.

Machine language: a set of binary-code instructions capable of being understood by a computer without translation.

Mainframe computer: a large-scale conventional computer, well below the capabilities of a supercomputer but with a processing speed about 100 times faster than that of a microcomputer.

Mantissa: the fractional part of a number expressed in floating-point notation.

Megaflops: one million floating-point operations per second.

Memory: the principal space inside a computer for storing instructions and data; multiple-processor systems may include both a central, or global, memory shared by all processors, and local memories associated with each individual processor.

Memory address: a numerically coded location in a computer's memory; in a program, data is usually referred to by its memory address.

Memory banks: partitioned units within a computer's memory that can work in sequence to supply the processor with a steady stream of data.

Microchip: *See* Integrated circuit.

Microcomputer: a desktop or portable computer, based on a microprocessor and meant for a single user; often called a personal computer.

Microprocessor: a single chip, or integrated circuit, containing all the elements of a computer's central processing unit.

Microsecond: a millionth of a second.

Minicomputer: a midsize, general-purpose computer that is capable of performing tasks similar to those of a supercomputer but at a slower rate; because they cost less, the most powerful minicomputers are an attractive alternative to supercomputers for certain processing chores.

MIPS: millions of instructions per second; used as a measure of processing speed for conventional computers and for supercomputers performing scalar processing.

Modeling: using supercomputers to simulate complex physical phenomena through the manipulation of mathematical equations that represent those phenomena.

MOSFET (metal-oxide semiconductor, field-effect transistor): a semiconductor switch consisting of three regions of semiconductor material called the source, the channel and the drain, with an electric field between source and drain controlling the flow of current.

Multicomputer: a computer architecture that incorporates more than one processor and both global and local memories.

Multiprocessor: a computer architecture incorporating multiple processors that must share access to a central, global memory.

Nanosecond: one billionth of a second.

N-type semiconductor: a semiconductor, such as silicon, containing traces of an impurity, such as phosphorus, that creates a surplus of electrons and improves conductivity.

Opcode: the part of an instruction that tells a computer what operation is to be performed; the word "opcode" is a contraction of "operating code."

Operand: the part of an instruction that gives the computer the memory address of the data to be processed.

Optical computing: an experimental technology in which information travels as a beam of light and the computer's switches are triggered by a flow of photons rather than electrons.

Optical switch: a semiconductor switch that is turned on or off by beams of light.

Overhead: in multiple-processor systems, delays caused by the necessity of coordinating the activities of several processors.

Parallel processing: any of several techniques, such as pipelining and vector processing, that involve the execution of more than one instruction or part of an instruction at the same time. In so-called massively parallel systems, multiple-processing units work simultaneously to solve problems.

Peripheral processor: a subsidiary processing element, such as an input/output controller or a coprocessor, that is designed to handle specialized tasks that would otherwise slow down the main processor.

Pipelining: a processing technique that allows a CPU or a processor to work on more than one instruction at a time, in assembly-line fashion. In its simplest form, pipelining involves fetching a new instruction from memory during each phase of the instruction cycle.

Program: a set of instructions for performing an operation or solving a problem by computer.

Protocol matching: the process of making two computer systems or networks compatible, by converting one system's governing rules, or protocols, into another's.

P-type semiconductor: a semiconductor containing traces of an impurity, such as aluminum, that creates holes (a deficiency of electrons); like electrons, holes can carry a current.

Real-time computing: computer processing rapid enough to solve problems and handle events as they occur.

Reconstitution overhead: in multiple-processor systems, the cost in time of merging partial results to achieve a final result.

Reduction machine: a supercomputer that reduces large problems into smaller operations that can then be executed simultaneously; partial results from multiple processors are combined until a final result is achieved.

Register: a small amount of directly accessible memory, often found within a computer's CPU.

Resolution: the accuracy of a computer simulation, or model; resolution increases in proportion to the amount of data on which the model is based.

Routing network: in multiprocessors and multicomputers, the communications system that allows processors to exchange data and that sets priorities when processor demands conflict.

Scalar processing: the conventional procedure for executing program instructions, requiring a separate instruction cycle for every operation.

SEED (self-electro-optic-effect device): an optical switch in which beams of light trigger electronic events that cause the light to be either transmitted or absorbed, thus turning the switch on or off.

Seismic imaging: the use of reflected sound waves to create a picture of rock layers below the surface of the earth and beneath the ocean floor.

Semiconductor: a solid crystalline substance whose electrical conductivity falls between that of a conductor and that of an insulator; the main material from which transistors and integrated circuits are made.

Semiconductor switch: the fundamental component of all electronic computers, composed of semiconductor material and capable of turning a current on or off; semiconductor switches store and transmit information expressed as zeros and ones.

Separation overhead: in multiple-processor systems, the cost in time of dividing a program for parallel processing.

Serial processing: the standard method of executing a program on a conventional, von Neumann computer, in which instructions are processed in a step-by-step, sequential fashion; opposed to parallel processing.

Source: in certain computer switches, the area of semiconductor material that supplies current-carrying electrons; equivalent to the emitter in a bipolar transistor.

Speed-matching: the process of adjusting data rates to correspond with the working speeds of various computer devices.

Staging disk: in a supercomputer center, a short-term external storage device for data generated by supercomputers and headed for either long-term storage or recording devices such as printers.

Substrate: in a transistor or integrated circuit, a foundation of semiconductor material.

Supercomputer: the term applied to the fastest, most powerful computers at a given time; supercomputers typically are used to solve scientific or industrial problems that involve the creation of mathematical models and the manipulation of large amounts of data.

Supercomputer center: a facility housing several supercomputers, along with support mechanisms such as storage and recording devices and communications equipment; the center allows many users to share access to supercomputer power.

Superconductor: a metal such as lead or niobium that, when cooled below a certain temperature, can conduct a current with no electrical resistance; superconductor switches control current flow with a magnetic field and consume very little power. *See also* Josephson junction.

Supercurrent: a current that can flow forever but that can only exist in superconductor switches cooled to near absolute zero.

Superlattice: in an optical switch, alternating layers of semiconductor materials that absorb or transmit certain wavelengths of light.

Token matching unit: the component of a dataflow computer that matches data tokens headed for the same instruction packet; if one token arrives early, the token matching unit will store it until its mate arrives.

Token queue: in a dataflow computer, a buffer that slows down data produced by processors for the less speedy token matching unit and input/output devices.

Transistor: a switching device that can amplify a voltage or turn a current on or off; made of semiconductor material and usually consisting of an emitter, a collector and a base.

Translator program: software that converts programs written in high-level languages into the binary code of machine language; translators are either interpreters, which convert instructions one at a time, or compilers, which translate an entire program before execution begins.

Truncation: the process of dropping digits from a number in order to fit it into the word size of a particular computer's circuits; floating-point notation helps reduce the need for truncation by using fewer digits to express a number.

Vacuum tube: the earliest form of electronic switch, eventually replaced by the transistor.

Vector processing: a parallel-processing technique in which an instruction is invoked once and then is executed on an entire list, or vector, of numbers.

Very-large-scale integrated (VLSI) circuit: a type of computer chip containing hundreds of thousands of transistors and other components on a single sliver of semiconductor material.

Von Neumann architecture: the conventional computer design, composed of a memory connected by a bus to a central processing unit that performs operations sequentially.

Von Neumann bottleneck: an operational slowdown in conventional computer designs, caused by the funneling of information into a single channel between the CPU and memory.

Word: the number of bits that a computer can store at a single memory location, treated by the computer as a unit; word size ranges from eight bits in a microcomputer to as many as 64 bits in a supercomputer.

Bibliography

Books

Carter, Alden R., and Wayne J. Leblanc, *Supercomputers.* New York: Watts, Franklin, 1985.

Chirlian, Paul M., *Understanding Computers.* Beaverton, Oreg.: Dilithium Press, 1978.

Curran, Susan, and Ray Curnow, *Overcoming Computer Illiteracy: A Friendly Introduction to Computers.* New York: Penguin Books, 1983.

Data Flow Computing. Chichester, England: Ellis Horwood, 1985.

Evans, David J., ed., *Parallel Processing Systems.* Cambridge: Cambridge University Press, 1982.

Feigenbaum, Edward A., and Pamela McCorduck, *The Fifth Generation: Artificial Intelligence and Japan's Computer Challenge to the World.* Reading, Mass.: Addison-Wesley, 1983.

Hockney, Roger W., and James W. Eastwood, *Computer Simulation Using Particles.* New York: McGraw-Hill, 1981.

Hord, R. Michael, *The ILLIAC IV: The First Supercomputer.* Rockville, Md.: Computer Science Press, 1982.

Hwang, Kai, *Supercomputer: Design and Applications.* Silver Spring, Md.: IEEE Computer Society Press, 1984.

Hwang, Kai, and Faye A. Briggs, *Computer Architecture and Parallel Processing.* New York: McGraw-Hill, 1984.

Jenkins, Richard, *Supercomputers of Today and Tomorrow: The Parallel Processing Revolution.* Blue Ridge Summit, Pa.: TAB Books, 1986.

Kuck, David J., *The Structure of Computers and Computations.* Vol. 1. New York: John Wiley & Sons, 1978.

Kuhn, Robert H., and David A. Padua, *Tutorial on Parallel Processing.* Silver Spring, Md.: IEEE Computer Society Press, 1981.

Lykos, Peter, and Isaiah Shavitt, *Supercomputers in Chemistry.* American Chemical Society, 1981.

McWhorter, Gene, *Understanding Digital Electronics.* Fort Worth, Tex.: Radio Shack, 1978.

Metropolis, Nicholas, ed., *Frontiers of Supercomputing.* Berkeley: University of California Press, 1986.

Moto-oka, T., ed., *Fifth Generation Computer Systems.* New York: North-Holland Publishing, 1982.

NEC Corporation: The First 80 Years. Tokyo: NEC Corporation, 1984.

Nelson, Roice H., *New Technologies in Exploration Geophysics.* Houston: Gulf Publishing, 1983.

Olsen, Kenneth H., *Digital Equipment Corporation: The First Twenty-Five Years.* New York: The Newcomen Society in North America, 1983.

Pampe, William R., *Petroleum: How It Is Found and Used.* Hillside, N.J.: Enslow Publishers, 1984.

Pauling, Linus, and Roger Hayward, *The Architecture of Molecules.* San Francisco: W. H. Freeman and Co., 1964.

Potter, J. L., ed., *The Massively Parallel Processor.* Cambridge: The MIT Press, 1985.

Rodrigue, Garry, ed., *Parallel Computations.* New York: Academic Press, 1982.

Siewiorek, Daniel P., *Parallel Processing Handbook.* Marlboro, Mass.: Encore Computer Corporation, 1986.

Siewiorek, Daniel P., C. Gordon Bell and Allen Newell, *Computer Structures: Principles and Examples.* New York: McGraw-Hill, 1982.

Smith, Jon M., *Mathematical Modeling and Digital Simulation for Engineers and Scientists.* New York: John Wiley & Sons, 1977.

Sobel, Robert, *I.B.M. Colossus in Transition.* New York: Bantam Books, 1981.

Torrero, Edward A., ed., *Next-Generation Computers.* New York: Institute of Electrical & Electronics Engineers, 1985.

Watson, J. D., *The Molecular Biology of the Gene.* New York: W. A. Benjamin, 1965.

Periodicals

Abraham, Eitan, Colin T. Seaton and S. Desmond Smith, "The Optical Computer." *Scientific American,* Feb. 1983.

Absar, Ilyas, "Applications of Supercomputer in the Petroleum Industry." *Simulation,* May 1985.

Aldag, John E., "Computer Graphics for Oil and Gas Exploration." *Cray Channels,* Vol. 5, No. 1.

Alexander, Tom:
"Cray's Way of Staying Super-Duper." *Fortune,* Mar. 18, 1985.
"Reinventing the Computer." *Fortune,* Mar. 5, 1984.

Assmann, Werner, and Erich Schelkle, "Examples of Computation Methods in Automotive Engineering." *Cray Channels,* fall 1985.

Baker, Tim, and Antony Jameson, "Computational Methods and Aerodynamics." *Cray Channels,* summer 1986.

Baldwin, William, "Through the Earth, Darkly." *Forbes,* Dec. 17, 1984.

Bell, Gordon, "The Future of High Performance Computers in Science and Engineering." *Communications of the ACM,* September 1989.

Benoit, Ellen, "Filling the Gap." *Forbes,* Mar. 11, 1985.

Boffey, Philip, "The Race for Computer Supremacy: Who's Ahead?" *The New York Times,* Oct. 23, 1984.

Boss, Alan, "Collapse and Formation of Stars." *Scientific American,* Jan. 1985.

Brody, Herb, "Ultrafast Chips at the Gate." *High Technology,* Mar. 1986.

Bylinsky, Gene, "What's Sexier and Speedier Than Silicon." *Fortune,* June 24, 1985.

Casasent, David, "Coherent Optical Computing." *IEEE Computer,* Jan. 1979.

Cohen, Charles L., "Japanese Supercomputers: They Haven't Taken Over Yet." *Electronics,* Apr. 7, 1986.

Colvin, Geoffrey, "The Astonishing Growth of DEC." *Fortune,* May 3, 1982.

Conaway, James, "Mr. Secret Weapon." *The Washington Post Magazine,* May 15, 1983.

Danielson, Richard D., "Cooling a Superfast Computer." *Electronic Packaging & Production,* July 1986.

Dennis, Kneale, "Which Computer Is Speediest? Measures May Be Misleading." *The Wall Street Journal,* Apr. 4, 1986.

Douglas, John H., "New Computer Architectures Tackle Bottleneck." *High Technology,* June 1983.

Farouki, Rida T., Stuart L. Shapiro and Saul A. Teukolsky, "Computational Astrophysics on the Array Processor." *IEEE Spectrum,* June 1983.

Feigenbaum, Edward, and Pamela McCorduck, "Land of the Rising Fifth Generation Computer." *High Technology,* June 1983.

Furst, Al, "Number-Crunching Pays Off for Floating Point Systems." *Electronic Business,* Nov. 1982.

"Giants in Small Packages." *IEEE Spectrum,* Feb. 1982.

Grubbs, Dean, "Computational Analysis in Automotive Design." *Cray Channels,* fall 1985.

Gullo, Karen:
"Straight and Narrow." *Datamation,* Aug. 1, 1985.
"Supercomputing in the Real World." *Datamation,* Oct. 1, 1986

Gurd, J. R., C. C. Kirkham and I. Watson, "The Manchester Prototype Dataflow Computer." *Communications of the ACM,* Jan. 1985.

Hallgren, Richard, "Hurricanes, Tornadoes: Is Worst Yet to Come?" *U.S. News & World Report,* June 17, 1985.

Hayes, Jim, "MOS Scaling." *IEEE Computer,* Jan. 1980.

Heppenheimer, T. A., "Aviation Industry's Aerodynamic Duo." *High Technology,* Apr. 1986.

Hittinger, William C., "Metal-Oxide-Semiconductor Technology." *Scientific American,* Aug. 1973.

Hwang, Kai, "Multiprocessor Supercomputers for Scientific/Engineering Applications." *Computer,* June 1985.

Lee, T. C., and Stephen Jamison, "Gallium Arsenide in Digital Electronics." *Scientific Honeyweller,* Apr. 1985.

Levine, Ronald D., "Supercomputers." *Scientific American,* Jan. 1982.

Maranto, Gina, "Are We Close to the Road's End?" *Discover,* Jan. 1986.

Matisoo, Juri, "The Superconducting Computer." *Scientific American,* May 1980.

Meindl, James D., "Microelectronic Circuit Elements." *Scientific American,* Sept. 1977

Mendez, Raul, and Steve Orszag, "The Japanese Supercomputer Challenge." *Datamation,* May 15, 1984.

Mills, Thomas G., "Gallium Arsenide Technology." *TRW Quest,* spring 1980.

"Minicomputers Challenge the Big Machines." *Business Week,* Apr. 26, 1976.

Mitchell, J. Murray, "Computers and the Weather." *Weatherwise,* Oct. 1983.

"New Breed of Computers Packs Punch." *The Boston Herald,* June 8, 1986.

"A New Strategy for No. 2 in Computers." *Business Week,* May 2, 1983.

Parker, Evan, and Richard King, "New Channels for Microchips." *New Scientist,* Oct. 14, 1982.

Pease, R.F.W., "Fabrication Issues for Next-Generation Circuits." *IEEE Spectrum,* Nov. 1983.

Petre, Peter, "America's Most Successful Entrepreneur." *Fortune,* Oct. 27, 1986.

Petzet, G. Alan, "Industry's Use of Computer Shows Big Increase." *Oil and Gas Journal,* Apr. 9, 1984.

Phillips, D. Howard, "GaAs Insulators." *Military Electronics/Countermeasures,* May 1980.

"The Race Is Not Always to the Gigafloppiest." *Economist,* April 15, 1989.

Raimondi, Donna, "From Code Busters to Mainframes: The History of CDC." *Computerworld,* July 15, 1985.

Riganati, John P., and Paul B. Schneck, "Supercomputing." *IEEE,* Oct. 1984.

Robinson, Arthur L.:
"Array Processors: Maxi Number Crunching for a Mini Price." *Science,* Jan. 12, 1979.
"Multiple Quantum Wells for Optical Logic." *Science,* Aug. 24, 1984.
"Problems with Ultraminiaturized Transistors." *Science,* June 13, 1980.

Rubbert, Paul E., "The Impact of Computational Methods on Aircraft Design." *Cray Channels,* Vol. 6, No. 4.

Sanger, David E., "The Surge in Supercomputers." *The New York Times,* Mar. 1, 1986.

Schatz, Willie, "Who's Winning the Supercomputer Race?" *Datamation,* July 15, 1989.

Schulbach, Catherine, "Putting the 'Super' in Supercomputers." *Aerospace America,* Aug. 1985.

"Selling Machine: Massively Parallel Computers." *Economist,* May 27, 1989.

Siebel, George, "Computational Chemistry of Biomacromolecules." *Cray Channels,* spring 1985.

Slotnick, D. L., "The Fastest Computer." *Scientific American,* Feb. 1971.

Smith, Desmond, and David Miller, "Computing at the Speed of Light." *New Scientist,* Feb. 21, 1980.

Smith, Peter W., and W. J. Tomlinson, "Bistable Optical Devices Promise Subpicosecond Switching." *IEEE Spectrum,* June 1981.

Smith, S. D., "Optical Bistability." *Spectrum,* 1980.

Stamps, David, "The Cray Style." *Corporate Report,* Dec. 1982.

"Supercomputers Come Out into the World." *Economist,* Aug. 11, 1984.

Teja, Ed, "New Architectures." *Computers & Electronics,* May 1984.

Thomsen, Dietrick E., "Schroedinger Goes to Monte Carlo." *Science News,* Aug. 23, 1986.

Tippee, Bob, "Technological Advances Yield Better Data from Seismic Surveys." *Oil & Gas Journal,* Oct. 3, 1983.

"Using Computers to Model the Atmosphere." *Weatherwise,* Oct. 1983.

Uttal, Bro, "Here Comes Computer Inc." *Fortune,* Oct. 4, 1982.

Washington, Warren M., and Gerald A. Meehl, "Seasonal Cycle Experiment on the Climate Sensitivity Due to a Doubling of CO_2 with an Atmospheric General Circulation Model Coupled to a Simple Mixed-Layer Ocean Model." *Journal of Geophysical Research,* Oct. 20, 1984.

Wellborn, Stanley N., "Science Takes On Tornadoes." *U.S. News & World Report,* May 12, 1986.

West, S. "Beyond the One-Track Mind." *Science 85,* Nov. 1985.

Wimmer, Erich, et al., "Computational Chemistry by Supercomputer." *Cray Channels,* winter 1986.

Wolfe, Alexander, "Optical Computing Is Beginning to Take On the Glow of Reality." *Electronics Week,* June 10, 1985.

Worlton, Jack, "Understanding Supercomputer Benchmarks." *Datamation,* Sept. 1, 1984.

Other Publications

Clark, Rockoff, and Associates, *The LINC Was Early and Small.* (monograph) New York: Association for Computing Machinery, 1986.

"Guide to the NMFECC Machine Room." Livermore, Calif.: Lawrence Livermore National Laboratory, June 1985.

Klemp, Joseph B., "Dynamics of Tornadic Thunderstorms." *Annual Review, Inc.,* 1987.

McMahon, Frank H., *The Livermore Fortran Kernels: A Computer Test of the Numerical Performance Range.* Livermore, Calif.: Lawrence Livermore National Laboratory, June 27, 1986.

Meehl, Gerald A., "Modeling the Earth's Climate." *Climate Change.* Hingham, Mass.: D. Reidel Publishing, 1984.

Microelectronics Research & Development — A Background Paper, OTA-BP-CIT-40. Washington, D.C.: U.S. Government Printing Office, Mar. 1986.

Miller, D.A.B., et al., "Integrated Quantum Well Self-Electro-Optic-Effect Device: 2x2 Array of Optically Bistable Switches." Unpublished manuscript.

National Center for Atmospheric Research, Annual Report-Fiscal Year 1984. Boulder, Colo.: University Corporation for Atmospheric Research & National Center for Atmospheric Research, 1985.

NCAR-The National Center for Atmospheric Research. Boulder, Colo.: The National Center for Atmospheric Research, no date.

Scace, Robert I., *Semiconductor Technology for the Non-Technologist.* Washington, D.C.: National Bureau of Standards, Jan. 1981.

Acknowledgments

The index for this book was prepared by Mel Ingber. The editors also wish to thank the following individuals and institutions for their help in the preparation of this volume: **In the United States:** California — Livermore: Robert R. Borchers, Pierre DuBois, Kirby Fong, Dieter Fuss, John Hallquist, Gordon Longerbeam, Frank McMahon, Samuel Mendicino, George A. Michael, John E. Ranelletti and Ronald V. Teunis, Lawrence Livermore National Laboratory; Moffett Field: Victor Peterson, Ames Research Center, National Aeronautics and Space Administration; San Diego: William Bennett, Supercomputer Center, University of California at San Diego; Colorado — Boulder: Julius Chang, Joan Frisch, Joseph Klemp, Gerald Meehl and Nita Razo, National Center for Atmospheric Research; Connecticut — Ridgefield: Indranil Chakravarty, Schlumberger-Doll Research; District of Columbia — Gordon Bell, National Science Foundation; Alan P. Boss, Carnegie Institution of Washington; James Decker, U.S. Department of Energy; Joan Winston, Office of Technology Assessment, U.S. Congress; Illinois — Champaign: William H. Allan, University of Illinois at Urbana-Champaign; Maryland — Greenbelt: Claire Parkinson, Goddard Space Flight Center, National Aeronautics and Space Administration; Rockville: John Wehrung, Gentronix; Massachusetts — Boston: Lynn Hall, The Computer Museum; Maynard: Stephen A. Kallis Jr., Digital Equipment Corporation; Minnesota — Mendota Heights: Vito Bongiorno and Erich Wimmer, Cray Research, Inc.; Minneapolis: Robert Chinn; Scott Jessee, Control Data Corporation; Robert H. Ewald, John Rollwagen, Kim Salisbury, Andrew Scott and Carol Smith, Cray Research, Inc.; New Jersey — Short Hills: Michael Jacobs, AT&T Bell Laboratories; New Mexico — Los Alamos: Dale C. Sparks, Los Alamos National Laboratory; New York — New York: Pat DiNapoli, Ammann & Whitney; Palisades: John Mutter, Lamont-Doherty Geological Observatory; Valhalla: Donald Kenny, IBM Corporation; North Carolina — Chapel Hill: Gyula Mago, University of North Carolina at Chapel Hill; Oregon — Beaverton: Norman Winningstad, Floating Point Systems, Inc.; Rhode Island — Providence: Thor Johnson, Telesis, Inc.; Texas — Austin: Harvey Cragon, University of Texas; Dallas: Frank Robl, Mobil Oil; Plano: Keith Strandtman, Arco Exploration Co.; The Woodlands: Olin Johnson, Houston Area Research Center; Virginia — Alexandria: Alan Bligh; Wisconsin — Chippewa Falls: Jerry Brost, Steve Hogseth and Dean Roush, Cray Research, Inc.

Picture Credits

Credits from left to right are separated by semicolons, from top to bottom by dashes.

Cover, 6: Art by Matt McMullen. 8: Robert Bonifield, courtesy The Computer Museum, Boston. 11: Courtesy IBM. 12: Courtesy Control Data Corporation. 15: Mark Sexton, courtesy The Computer Museum, Boston. 17: Courtesy Control Data Corporation. 19: Art by Steve Bauer/Bill Burrows Studio. 20, 21: Art by Steve Bauer/Bill Burrows Studio; University of Illinois at Urbana-Champaign — Morton S. Weiss, Lawrence Livermore National Laboratory(5). 22, 23: Art by Steve Bauer/Bill Burrows Studio — National Aeronautics and Space Administration; National Aeronautics and Space Administration — Courtesy Lockheed-Georgia Company. 24, 25: Burns and Roe Enterprises, Inc.; Ammann & Whitney Consulting Engineers; courtesy of Peugeot S.A. Group, produced on a Cray X-MP supercomputer at Cray Research, Inc., Minneapolis. 26, 27: Art by Steve Bauer/Bill Burrows Studio; Cray Research, Inc.; A. Winchester and K. Hara, Reservoir Modeling Engineering, Nipon Schlumberger KK, Tokyo. 28, 29: Alan Boss, Carnegie Institution of Washington. 30: Art by Matt McMullen. 35-37: Art by Peter Sawyer. 42, 43: Art by William J. Hennessy Jr. and John Drummond. 44, 45: Courtesy Lawrence Livermore Laboratory—art by William J. Hennessy Jr. and John Drummond. 46, 47: Art by William J. Hennessy Jr. and Matt McMullen. 48: Cray Research, Inc. 49-66: Art by Matt McMullen. 70: Courtesy Digital Equipment Corporation. 73: Courtesy Digital Equipment Corporation. 77: National Center for Atmospheric Research/National Science Foundation. 78, 79: Art by Lloyd K. Townsend(2); National Center for Atmospheric Research. 80, 81: Art by Lloyd K. Townsend. 82-86: National Center for Atmospheric Research/National Science Foundation. 87: Art by Lloyd K. Townsend. 88: Art by Matt McMullen. 92-95: Art by Stephen Wagner. 96, 97: Fil Hunter, courtesy Grace Murray Hopper. 99-101: Art by Al Kettler. 104: Courtesy The Computer Museum, Boston. 107-115: Art by Stephen Wagner. 116, 117: Diagrams by John Drummond—art by Stephen Wagner. 118, 119: Art by Stephen Wagner.

Index

Numerals in italics indicate an illustration of the subject mentioned.

A

Aircraft design, 19, *22-23*, 44
Alliant FX/8, 98
American Research & Development (ARD), 69
Anderson, Harlan, 68, 69
Animation, film, 44
Architecture, computer, 33; massively parallel, 97-98, 102-104, 105-106; modified von Neumann, *52-65;* non-von Neumann, 49, 89-106; parallel, 33-34, 49, *54-65,* 97-98, 102-104, 105-106; von Neumann, 33, 49, *50-53,* 97, 98, 106
ARCO, 44
Array processors (AP), 73-76; uses, 75, 76
Artificial Intelligence (AI) and supercomputers, 89, 97, 103-106
Astrophysical research, 19, *28-29,* 74-75
Automobile design, 19, *25*

B

Bell, Gordon, 70
Black holes, 74, 75
Burroughs Corporation, 33; ILLIAC IV 34, 97
Bus, computer, and speed, 51

C

California Institute of Technology, 102
Carnegie Mellon, 90
Cedar system, 98, 102
Central processing unit (CPU), *50-53;* coprocessor, *57;* multiple functional units, *56-57;* pipelined, *58-59*
Chemical transport models, *82-83*
Chen, Steve, 41, 48, 98
Chevron Geosciences Co., 7
Climate. *See* Meteorology, computer modeling
Clock, and speed, *51*
Computational chemistry, *20-21*
Computer modeling. *See* Computational chemistry; Finite-element analysis; Meteorology
Computer, principal components, *50*
Concentrators, *46*
Connection Machine, 103-105
Control Data Corporation (CDC), 11, 14-17, 31-32, 34, 44, 96; CDC 1604, 11, 14, 16; CDC 3600, *12;* CDC 6600, 14, *15-17, 35,* 48; CDC 7600, 18, 48; Cyber 203, 44, 89; Cyber 205, 44, 90; and IBM, 16, 18; Star-100, 33, 34, 39
Cooling systems, *35-37*
Coprocessor, mathematical, *57*

Cornell University, 74, 75, 90
Cosmic Cube, 102, 104
Cray Computers, 48
Cray Research, 32-33, 39, 41, 45, 48, 96; Cray-1, *36,* 38-39, 42, 89; Cray-2, *37, 45, 46,* 97, 104; Cray-3, 45, 48; Quarter Horse, 45; X-MP, 7, 41, 44, *46,* 48, 90, 97, 104; X-MP/48, 22, 23, 97; Y-MP, *46,* 48, 97
Cray, Seymour R., 14, 15, *17,* 18, 31-33, 38-39, 41, 44, 45, *48,* 96, 98
Culler, Glen, 74

D

Dataflow architecture, *99-101,* 102-103; Sigma 1, 106
Data General, 71
Defense Advanced Research Projects Agency (DARPA), 90, 106
Dennis, Jack, 103
Depth migration, *27*
Digital Equipment Corporation (DEC), 67-72; employees, *70;* and inexpensive computers, 67; PDP-1, 67, 70; PDP-8, 71, *73;* PDP-11, 71; production, *73*
Digital Productions, 44
Diode, junction, *109*
Doriot, Georges, 69, 70
Dunwell, Stephen, 10, *11*

E

Engineering Research Associates (ERA), 11-13, 31; Atlas, 12; ERA 1101, 12-13
Engstrom, Howard, 12
ETA Systems, 44, 45, 48, 96-97

F

Fifth Generation project, 89-91, 97
Finite-element analysis, *24-25*
Floating-point arithmetic, *40*
Floating Point Systems, 72-74, 75-76; AP-120B, 73-74; AP-190L, 74; scientific computers, 76
Fluid dynamics, 19, *22-23*
Fox, Geoffrey, 102
Fujitsu, 45, 96; VP-400, 91; VP-2600, 97

G

Gallium arsenide (GaAs), 45, 107, *112-113, 118-119*
Gulfstream Aerospace Corporation, 44

H

Hallquist, John, 44
Hillis, Daniel, 103-105, *104*
Hitachi, 45, 91, 97; S810-20, 91
Hopper, Grace Murray, 96
Houston Area Research Center (HARC), 96

I

IBM, 8, 16, 96; Model 90, 16, 17-18; IBM 370/168, 75; IBM 704, 9, 10, 11; IBM 3081, 76; pipelining, 33; and SAGE, 68; and Stretch, 9, *11;* and Supercomputer Systems, Inc., 48; vector processor experiment, 45
ILLIAC IV (Illinois Automatic Computer), 34, 97
Image analysis applications, 105
Input/output processor, *54;* and speed, 51
Instruction cycles, 51, *52-53*
Intel, iPSC, 102

J

Japanese supercomputers, 89-91, 96, 97; dataflow, 106; Fifth Generation project, 89-91, 98; MITI, 89, 90; National Superspeed computer project, 89, 91; structure of industry, 90-91
Johnson, Olin, 96
Josephson junctions, *114-115*

K

Kuck, David, 98, 102, 106

L

LARC (Livermore Advanced Research Computer), 8-9, 11
Lawrence Livermore National Laboratory, 8, 14, 41, 44, 45
Los Alamos Scientific Laboratory, 8, 9, 41
Lucas, Edouard, 7
Lukoff, Herman, 9

M

Magó, Gyula, 103, 104
Mathematical processors, 72, 74; advantages, 67
Memory: banks, 54, *55;* cache, 54, *55;* and speed, 51, 97, 98
Memory, magnetic core, 10; and Whirlwind, 68
Memory Test Computer (MTC), 68
Meteorology, computer modeling, *77, 78-87;* and acid rain, *82-83;* general circulation models (GCMs), *78-79;* simulation of climate changes, *80-81;* thunderstorms and tornadoes, *84-85*
Military applications, 8, 43, *44,* 105
MIMD (multiple instruction/multiple data), 104
Minicomputers: advantages, 67; inexpensive, 67, 70, 75; minisupers, 76; PDP, 70, 71; superminis, 76; uses, 71-72
Ministry of International Trade and Industry (MITI), Japanese, 89-91; Fifth Generation project, 89, 91, 98; National Superspeed computer project, 89, 91, 96

M.I.T., 67-69; Digital Computer Laboratory, 67-68
Molecular studies, *20-21*
Moto-oka, Tohru, 89
MRJ, Inc., 105
Multicomputer, *65*
Multiprocessor, *64-65*

N
National Aeronautics and Space Administration (NASA), 34, 105
National Center for Atmospheric Research (NCAR), 80
National Science Foundation, supercomputing centers, 90
NEC (Nippon Electric Company), 45, 91; SX-2, 91, 96; SX-3, 97
NON-VON, 106
Norris, William, *12,* 13-14, 16-17, 18, 31, 32
Nuclear processes, 8, *20-21,* 42

O
Oceanography, 19
Oil exploration, *7, 26-27, 43-44, 73-74*
O'Leary, George, 74
Olsen, Kenneth, 67-69, *70, 71*
Optical switches, *116-119*
Overhead, parallel processing, 93

P
Parallel architectures, 33-34, 49, 96-98; Cedar, 98, 102; coordinating, *92-95;* dataflow, *99-101,* 102-103; hypercube, 102; incorporation of, 97; large and small grain, 97, 103, 106; massively, 97-98, 102, 103-104, 105-106; overhead, 93; programming, 97-98; reduction, 103
Parafrase, 98
Parker, John E., 12
Perkin-Elmer, 105
Physics applications, 102
Pipelining, 33, *58-59,* 61, 74, *94,* 97
Pollution, modeling effects of, 78-79, *80-81, 82-83*

Prime numbers, *7;* mechanical number sieve, *8*
Princeton University, 90

R
Reduction architecture, 102, 103
Remington Rand: and ERA, 13; and Sperry, 13
Rollwagen, John, 41, 48, 91, 96, 106
Routing network, *64-65*

S
SAGE (Semi-Automatic Ground Environment), 68
Scalar processing, 33, 61
Scientific studies, 19, *20-29*
Seismic analysis, *7, 26-27, 43-44, 73-74*
Seitz, Charles, 102
Self-electro-optic-effect device (SEED), *118-119*
Semiconductors: gallium arsenide vs. silicon, 112; optical, *118-119;* structure and function, *108-109*
Service Bureau Corporation, 18
Shapiro, Stuart, 74, 75
Shaw, David Elliot, 106
SIMD (single instruction/multiple data), 104
Slaughter, Edward, 102
Sperry Rand—Univac Division, 8, 13; UNIVAC 1, *7;* UNIVAC 1103, 31; LARC, 8-9
Stretch, *9-11,* 16
Stunt boxes, 72
Supercomputer Systems, Inc., 48
Supercomputers: access to, 90; and array processors, 75; centers for, *46-47,* 90; early history, 8-18; growth of market, 43-44; increased competition, 44-45; speed comparisons, *42-45,* 91; strategies for increasing speed, 33, 49, *54-65;* uses, 7-8, 43-44; world reaction to Japanese challenge, 89-90
Superconductors in computers, *114-115*
Switches, 107; junction diode, *109;* and new semiconductors, *112-113;* optical, *116-119;* superconducting, *114-115;*

transistor, *110-113*
Switching network, crossbar, *64*

T
Taylor, Norman, 68
Tektronix, 72
Teukolsky, Saul, 74, 75
Texas Instruments, 33; ASC (Advanced Scientific Computer), 34, 39; DDP (Distributed Data Processor), 103
Thinking Machines Corporation, 104-105
Tinkertoy computer, *104*
Transistors: bipolar, *110;* gallium arsenide, *113;* HEMT, *113;* MOSFET, *110-111;* and supercomputers, 9, 10
TX-O, 68

U
United States, reaction to Japanese challenge, 89-90
UNIVAC (Universal Automatic Computer). *See* Sperry Rand
University of California at San Diego, 90
University of Illinois, 34, 90, 98
University of Pittsburgh, 90
University of Southwestern Louisiana, 103
University of Tokyo, 91
UNIX operating system, 97, 98

V
Vector processing, 33-34, *60-61*
Very-large-scale integration (VLSI), 97
Von Neumann, John, 33, 49. *See also* Architecture, computer

W
Watanabe, Tadashi, 91, 96
Watson, Thomas J., Jr., 10, 11, 16
Weapons research, 8, 42, *44*
Weather. *See* Meteorology, computer modeling
Whirlwind, 67-68
Wilson, Kenneth, 74, 75, 76
Winningstad, Norman, 72, 73, 75, 76
Wire length, and flow of electrical pulses, 39, 96-97

Time-Life Books Inc.
is a wholly owned subsidiary of
THE TIME INC. BOOK COMPANY

President and Chief Executive Officer: Kelso F. Sutton
President, Time Inc. Books Direct:
Christopher T. Linen

TIME-LIFE BOOKS INC.

EDITOR: George Constable
Director of Design: Louis Klein
Director of Editorial Resources: Phyllis K. Wise
Director of Photography and Research:
John Conrad Weiser

PRESIDENT: John M. Fahey Jr.
Senior Vice Presidents: Robert M. DeSena,
Paul R. Stewart, Curtis G. Viebranz, Joseph J. Ward
Vice Presidents: Stephen L. Bair, Bonita L.
Boezeman, Mary P. Donohoe, Stephen L. Goldstein,
Andrew P. Kaplan, Trevor Lunn, Susan J. Maruyama,
Robert H. Smith
New Product Development: Trevor Lunn,
Donia Ann Steele
Supervisor of Quality Control: James King

PUBLISHER: Joseph J. Ward

Editorial Operations
Production: Celia Beattie
Library: Louise D. Forstall

Computer Composition: Deborah G. Tait (Manager),
Monika D. Thayer, Janet Barnes Syring, Lillian Daniels

Correspondents: Elisabeth Kraemer-Singh (Bonn);
Christine Hinze (London); Christina Lieberman (New
York); Maria Vincenza Aloisi (Paris); Ann Natanson
(Rome). Valuable assistance was also provided by:
Dick Berry (Tokyo); Elizabeth Brown (New York).

UNDERSTANDING COMPUTERS

SERIES DIRECTOR: Roberta Conlan
Series Administrator: Loretta Britten

Editorial Staff for *Speed and Power*
Designer: Robert K. Herndon
Associate Editors: Peter Pocock, Lydia Preston (text),
Jeremy Ross (pictures)
Researchers:
Patti H. Cass
Esther Ferington
Gregory M. McGruder
Writers:
Allan Fallow
Robert M. S. Somerville
Assistant Designer: Christopher M. Register
Editorial Assistant: Miriam P. Newton
Copy Coordinator: Vilasini Balakrishnan
Picture Coordinator: Renée DeSandies

Special Contributors: Ronald H. Bailey, Martin
Baldessari, Edward Dolnick, Donal Kevin Gordon,
Brian P. Hayes, Carollyn James, Richard A. Jenkins,
Martin Mann, John I. Merritt, Valerie Moolman,
Anthony K. Pordes, Jeffrey Rothfeder, Charles C.
Smith, Joel Solkoff (text); Isabel Fucigna, Ann Miller,
Carol S. Nicotera, Roxie France Nuriddin, Beth Ann
Smith (research)

THE CONSULTANTS

GWEN BELL is director of Exhibitions and Collections at
The Computer Museum in Boston.

BRIAN HAYES has written on aspects of computing and
programming languages for *Scientific American, Computer Language, BYTE* and *The New York Times.*

NEIL McELROY, former head of the computer center at
the White Oak Laboratory of the Naval Surface Weapons
Center, directs the Communications, Control and Audio
Group at Avelex in Maryland.

JAMES R. McGRAW works for Lawrence Livermore National Laboratory, where his research focuses on writing
highly parallel programs for multiprocessor computers.
He is one of the principal designers of SISAL, a language
used by research groups on a variety of multiprocessors.

ISABEL NIRENBERG has dealt with a wide range of computer applications, from the analysis of data collected by
the Pioneer space probes to the matching of children and
families for adoption agencies. She works in the Computer Center of the State University of New York at Albany.

JOHN P. RIGANATI is director of Systems Research at the
Supercomputing Research Center in Lanham, Maryland.
His research interests include high-level languages, compilers, operating systems, metrics and technologies for
high-performance computing.

ROBERT I. SCACE has worked in the semiconductor field
since 1954 and is now the deputy director of the National
Bureau of Standards' Center for Electronics and Electrical
Engineering.

STUART L. SHAPIRO is coordinator of the Particle Simulation Group at Cornell University's Center for Theory
and Simulation in Science and Engineering. He also
serves as chairman of the school's Astronomy and Space
Sciences Colloquium.

DANIEL SIEWIOREK, a professor of computer science
and electrical and computer engineering at Carnegie
Mellon, has contributed to the design of nine multiprocessor systems. His research interests include parallel
processing and computer architecture, in addition to design automation.

REVISIONS STAFF

EDITOR: Lee Hassig

Designer: Robert K. Herndon
Writer: Esther Ferington
Assistant Designer: Bill McKenney
Copy Coordinators: Donna Carey, Anne Farr
Picture Coordinator: Leanne Miller

Consultants:
William P. Bennett is principal scientist at the San Diego
Supercomputer Center, University of California at San
Diego.

Michael R. Williams, a professor of computer science at
the University of Calgary in Canada, wrote *A History of
Computing Technology.*

Library of Congress Cataloging in Publication Data

Main entry under title:
Speed and power / by the editors of Time-Life Books.
    p.   cm.   (Understanding computers)
    Includes bibliographical references and index.
    1. Supercomputers. 2. Parallel processing (Electronic computers)
I. Time-Life Books. II. Series
QA76.5.S65893 1990   004' .35—dc20
                                        90-11079 CIP

ISBN 0-8094-7586-3 (hard cover)
ISBN 0-8094-7587-1 (library ed.)

For information on and a full description of any Time-Life Books
series listed, please call 1-800-621-7026 or write:
Reader Information
Time-Life Customer Service
P.O. Box C-32068
Richmond, Virginia 23261-2068

© 1990, 1987 Time-Life Books Inc. All rights reserved.
No part of this book may be reproduced in any form or by any
electronic or mechanical means, including information storage
and retrieval devices or systems, without prior written permission
from the publisher, except that brief passages may be quoted for
reviews.
Revised edition 1990. First printing. Printed in U.S.A.
Published simultaneously in Canada.
School and library distribution by Silver Burdett Company,
Morristown, New Jersey.

TIME-LIFE is a trademark of Time Warner Inc. U.S.A.